SHORT WALKS DARTMOOR NORTH
OKEHAMPTON AND CHAGFORD

by Steve Davison

View looking north from Scarey Tor

CONTENTS

Using this guide.. 4
Route summary table 6
Map key 7
Introduction.. 9
   Walking on North Dartmoor 9
   Where to stay.. 11
   Travel 11

The walks

1.	Sourton Tors	13
2.	Meldon Reservoir	17
3.	High Willhays and Yes Tor	23
4.	Cullever Steps	29
5.	Belstone and Belstone Common	35
6.	Kestor Rock and Scorhill Down	41
7.	Chagford and Meldon Hill	47
8.	Fernworthy Reservoir	53
9.	River Teign	59
10.	Three Reservoirs..	65
11.	Bovey Valley Woods and Lustleigh	69
12.	Grimspound and Bennett's Cross	75
13.	Bellever Tor	79
14.	Widecombe in the Moor...................................	85
15.	Haytor Rocks	91

Useful information... 95

USING THIS GUIDE

Routes in this book

In this book you will find a selection of easy or moderate walks suitable for almost everyone, including casual walkers and families with children, or for when you only have a short time to fill. The routes have been carefully chosen to allow you to explore the area and its attractions. Most routes are circular or out-and-back, although some linear walks may be included that use public transport to get back to the start. Although there may be some climbs there is no challenging terrain, but do bear in mind that conditions can sometimes be wet or muddy underfoot. A route summary table is included on page 6 to help you choose the right walk.

Clothing and footwear

You won't need any special equipment to enjoy these walks. The weather in Britain can be changeable, so choose clothing suitable for the season and wear or carry a waterproof jacket. For footwear, comfortable walking boots or trainers with a good grip are best. A small rucksack for drinks, snacks and spare clothing is useful. See www.adventuresmart.uk.

Walk descriptions

At the beginning of each walk you'll find all the information you need:

- start/finish location, with a what3words address to help you find it
- parking and transport information, estimated walking time, total distance and climb
- details of public toilets available along the route and where you can get refreshments
- a summary of the key highlights of the walk and what you might see

Timings given are the time to complete the walk at a reasonable walking pace. Allow extra time for extended stops or if walking with children.

The route is described in clear, easy-to-follow directions, with each waypoint marked on an accompanying map extract. It's a good idea to read the whole of the route instructions before setting out, so that you know what to expect.

Maps, GPX files and what3words

Extracts from the OS® 1:25,000 map accompany each route. GPX files for all the walks in this book are available to download at www.cicerone.co.uk/1191/gpx.

What3words is a free smartphone app which identifies every 3m square of the globe with a unique three-word address, e.g. ///destiny.cafe.sonic. For more information see https://what3words.com/products/what3words-app.

USING THIS GUIDE

Walking with children

Even young children can be surprisingly strong walkers, but every family is different and you may need to adapt the timings given in this book to take that into account. Make sure you go at the pace of the slowest member and choose a walk with an exciting objective in mind, such as a cave, river, waterfall or picnic spot. Many of the walks can be shortened to suit – suggestions are included at the end of the route description.

Dogs

Sheep or cattle may be found grazing on a number of these walks. Keep dogs under control at all times so that they don't scare or disturb livestock or wildlife. Cattle, particularly cows with calves, may very occasionally pose a risk to walkers with dogs. If you ever feel threatened by cattle, you should let go of your dog's lead and let it run free.

Enjoying the countryside responsibly

Enjoy the countryside and treat it with respect to protect our natural environments. Stick to footpaths and take your litter home with you. When driving, slow down on rural roads and park considerately, or better still use public transport. For more details check out www.gov.uk/countryside-code.

The Countryside Code

Respect everyone
- be considerate to those living in, working in and enjoying the countryside
- leave gates and property as you find them
- do not block access to gateways or driveways when parking
- be nice, say hello, share the space
- follow local signs and keep to marked paths unless wider access is available

Protect the environment
- take your litter home – leave no trace of your visit
- do not light fires and only have BBQs where signs say you can
- always keep dogs under control and in sight
- dog poo – bag it and bin it – any public waste bin will do
- care for nature – do not cause damage or disturbance

Enjoy the outdoors
- check your route and local conditions
- plan your adventure – know what to expect and what you can do
- enjoy your visit, have fun, make a memory

ROUTE SUMMARY TABLE

WALK NAME	START POINT	TIME	DISTANCE
1. Sourton Tors	Sourton	2hr	5.5km (3½ miles)
2. Meldon Reservoir	Meldon Reservoir	2¾hr	8km (5 miles)
3. High Willhays and Yes Tor	Rowtor car park	3½hr	10.5km (6½ miles)
4. Cullever Steps	Okehampton railway station	3hr	9.5km (6 miles)
5. Belstone and Belstone Common	Belstone	2hr	6.5km (4 miles)
6. Kestor Rock and Scorhill Down	Scorhill car park	2¾hr	8.5km (5¼ miles)
7. Chagford and Meldon Hill	Chagford	1¾hr	5km (3 miles)
8. Fernworthy Reservoir	Fernworthy Reservoir	2½hr	7.5km (4¾ miles)
9. River Teign	Fingle Bridge	2hr	6.5km (4 miles)
10. Three Reservoirs	Trenchford Reservoir car park	2hr	6km (3¾ miles)
11. Bovey Valley Woods and Lustleigh	Pullabrook car park	2½hr	8km (5 miles)
12. Grimspound and Bennett's Cross	Warren House Inn on B3212	2hr	6.5km (4 miles)
13. Bellever Tor	Postbridge Visitor Centre	2¼hr	7km (4¼ miles)
14. Widecombe in the Moor	Widecombe in the Moor	2¼hr	6.5km (4 miles)
15. Haytor Rocks	Haytor Visitor Centre	1¾hr	5km (3 miles)

ROUTE SUMMARY TABLE

HIGHLIGHTS
Tor, views, former railway, viaduct
Reservoir, woodland, tor, views
Tors, views, high open moor
Woodland, riverside, open moor
Village, tors, views, open moor, prehistoric relics
Prehistoric relics, tor, views, open moor
Town, tor, views
Reservoir, woodland, prehistoric relics
Wooded valley, riverside, castle
Reservoirs, woodland
Woodland, riverside, village
Prehistoric relics, open moor, tor, views, pub
Woodland, prehistoric relics, tor, views
Village, open moor, views
Tor, quarries, views, tramway

SYMBOLS USED ON ROUTE MAPS

S Start point

F Finish point

SF Start and finish at the same place

 Waypoint

 Route line

MAPPING IS SHOWN AT A SCALE OF 1:25,000

DOWNLOAD THE GPX FILES FOR FREE AT
www.cicerone.co.uk/1191/gpx

The stone row and cist on Lakehead Hill (Walk 13)

INTRODUCTION

The West Okement River on the way towards Black-a-Tor Copse (Walk 2)

Dartmoor, a national park since 1951, is a wild, and at times isolated, upland area tucked in the south-western corner of Devon, in south-west England. It is a land of blanket bogs, grass moors dotted with fascinating tors, tumbling streams crossed by old stone clapper bridges, and a diverse range of wildlife. Several millennia ago our ancestors left behind a fascinating treasure trove, from intriguing stone rows, to ancient stones circles and burial cairns (there's over 1500 of them), and over 5000 hut circles. But there are also the stark ruins of Dartmoor's mining heritage, and picturesque villages and hamlets that are home to cosy pubs and historic buildings.

Yes, the weather can be inclement at times, low cloud and mist can obscure the views and the high rainfall leads to numerous bogs and mires, but this climate also brings with it fascinating woodlands clothed in moss and lichen like some enchanted land.

Walking on North Dartmoor

The area covered by this guide encompasses the northern half of Dartmoor, roughly anywhere north of a line drawn from Tavistock in the west to Heathfield near Newton Abbot in the east. The walks are designed to show the varied nature of Dartmoor, from the high open moors dotted with craggy tors to tranquil woodland and riverside paths. Some of the walks follow sections of two long-distance routes: the Dartmoor Way and the Two Moors Way.

Hookney Tor (Walk 12)

The routes are generally well signposted, except on the open moor where there is little in the way of signage, and they all follow fairly well-used paths. They can be enjoyed all year round; however, some of the paths may be wet and rather muddy, especially during the winter months, and some of the walks have streams to cross with no footbridges. The temperature and weather can change quickly on the open moor, so it is always a good idea to carry some extra clothing, including a waterproof jacket, just in case.

The walks, which are all circular, explore many interesting places across northern Dartmoor, including Haytor Rocks (Walk 15) – probably Dartmoor's most well-known tor; the fascinating ancient relics at Grimspound (Walk 12) and Scorhill (Walk 6); the rare oak woodland of Black-a-Tor Copse (Walk 2); and picturesque towns and villages such as Chagford (Walk 7), Widecombe in the Moor (Walk 14) and Lustleigh (Walk 11). There is also a more challenging route (Walk 3) that visits High Willhays and Yes Tor – the two highest tors on Dartmoor and in southern England.

The joys of walking on Dartmoor are many. Sit for a while atop a craggy tor and admire the wonderful views while listening to nature's music, from skylarks singing high above to the wind whispering over the moor. Look for wildlife, enjoy a picnic, or explore the ancient sites – from stone circles to stone rows – and wonder as to their purpose. But most of all, enjoy and respect the unique landscape, character and wildlife of Dartmoor.

Where to stay

There is a wide range of accommodation across Dartmoor, from campsites and youth hostels to pubs with rooms and hotels, both within and just outside the national park.

The main bases in the northern half of the national park that offer a range of facilities – such as shops, pubs and accommodation – are Chagford, Lydford, Moretonhampstead, South Zeal and Widecombe in the Moor. Outside the national park there are several larger towns including Crediton and Okehampton (both offering rail services), Bovey Tracey and Tavistock.

Travel

The most useful railway stations for reaching the northern half of Dartmoor are Exeter, Newton Abbot, Plymouth and Okehampton, with good connections to London, South Wales, the Midlands and the North. There are no train stations within Dartmoor National Park.

Several of the walks in the guidebook start at, or near, public transport links, as detailed in the walk information. Useful bus services include Exeter to Okehampton; Exeter to Moretonhampstead via Drewsteignton and Chagford; Newton Abbot to Okehampton via Lustleigh and Chagford; Newton Abbot to Tavistock via Postbridge; and Tavistock to Okehampton via Sourton. There are also more local bus services, but these may be quite infrequent.

If travelling by car, Dartmoor is within easy reach from the M5 motorway in Devon via the A30 and A38. The national park is surrounded by a good road network including the A30 along the northern edge, the A386 along the western edge and the A38 on the eastern side. The B3212 crosses Dartmoor from Dunsford to Yelverton; another route crosses from Ashburton to Tavistock. Extending off these main routes is a network of narrow lanes, often with passing places.

The speed limit on all parts of the open moor is 40mph, reducing to 30mph in places. On the open moor, ponies, sheep and cattle roam freely so extra care is required, especially at night. All accidents with stock animals must be reported to the Livestock Protection Officer (see 'Useful information'). Only park in designated car parks or where on-street parking is allowed and never block access points.

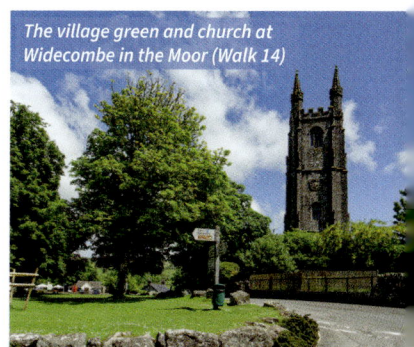

The village green and church at Widecombe in the Moor (Walk 14)

The Church of St Thomas a Becket and the Sourton Labyrinth

WALK 1
Sourton Tors

Start/finish	*Sourton village green*
Locate	*///dilute.calculate.never*
Cafes/pubs	*Pub at Sourton, pub at Lake (500m off route)*
Transport	*Buses between Okehampton and Tavistock stop at Sourton*
Parking	*Opposite Sourton village hall, off A386 (EX20 4HN)*
Toilets	*No public toilets on route*

From Sourton the walk sets out past the church and crosses over the Granite Way. Once on the open moor you make a steady climb up past the disused ice works to Sourton Tors – a great picnic spot with a view. From here you continue over the open moor making a sweeping descent of Lake Down towards Lake Viaduct. The final part of the walk follows the Granite Way back to Sourton. A shorter walk is also possible.

Time 2hr
Distance 5.5km (3½ miles)
Climb 230m

A shorter walk on the western edge of Dartmoor, visiting a Saxon cross, a church, a tor with a view and a viaduct

Lake Viaduct, now part of the Granite Way

SHORT WALKS DARTMOOR NORTH

The standing stone or cross at Sourton

1 From the village green and standing stone at **Sourton**, with your back to the Highwayman Inn, walk up the lane (Dartmoor Way and bridleway) heading away from the A386 and the pub. The Saxon standing stone, or cross, is known as the OXO stone due to the carving of two circles and a cross on the side facing the road.

Walk past the village hall and parking area, then continue up the track, with the **church** over to the left. At the junction with a gate on the left, keep ahead up the track, crossing the bridge over the former railway – now the **Granite Way**. Go through a gate onto the open moor and continue up the grassy track. When the walls on either side curve away, keep ahead to a cross-junction at the base of the steeper, boulder-strewn slope.

2 Follow the grassy track diagonally left uphill, with rock outcrops up to the right. As the boulders on the right peter out, turn right up a grassy path, passing the earth banks of the old 19th-century ice works. These were developed to make ice during the winter in series of shallow rectangular ponds; the venture only lasted for 10 years. Continue up a grassy path to the trig point on **Sourton Tors** (440m).

The trig point on Sourton Tors looking west

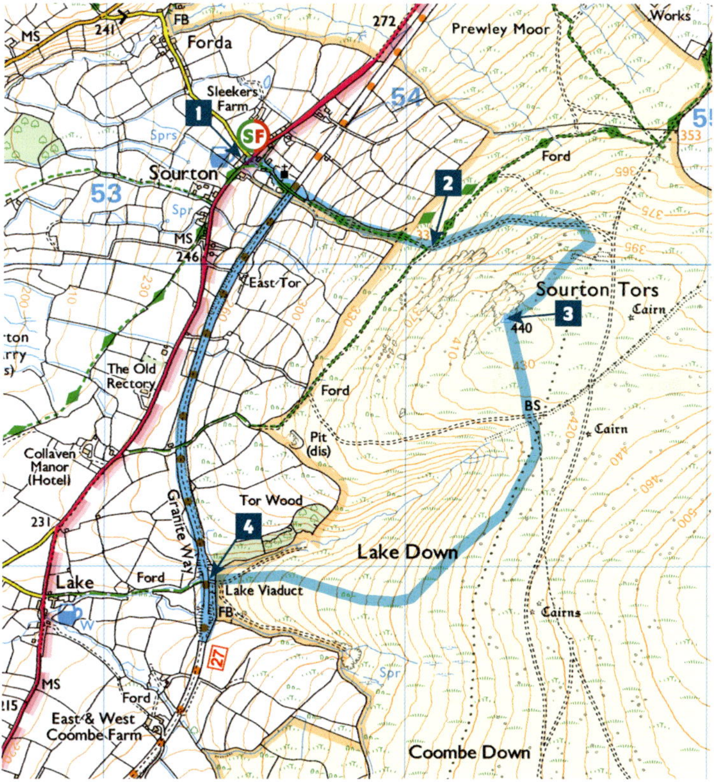

WALK 1 – SOURTON TORS

Sourton Tors makes a good picnic spot with views that include the rolling fields of Cornwall (west) and Devon (north), Meldon Reservoir (north-east) and West Mill Tor, Yes Tor and High Willhays (east).

3 Bear half-left gently downhill – aiming for Great Links Tor on the horizon – to a cross-path junction just before reaching a dip, near the top of a steep-sided valley. For the shorter walk turn right at this junction. Keep ahead for 100m to a Y-junction and fork right to follow a wide grassy path gently downhill, keeping above and left of the steep-sided valley. Follow the path as it curves right and descends **Lake Down** more steeply,

15

Following the Granite Way towards Sourton

aiming for the **Lake Viaduct** to a gate leaving the open moor.

4 Go through the gate, keep ahead for a few paces and before the viaduct turn left through a small gate (500m straight on is the hamlet of Lake and a pub). Continue parallel with the viaduct on your right, cross a bridge and head up the tarmac track to join the **Granite Way**.

> Lake Viaduct, built in 1874, was on the former railway line between Okehampton and Bere Alston. Part of this now forms the 18km-long Granite Way, a multi-use route (NCN 27) between Okehampton and Lydford.

Turn right along the tarmac track for 1.5km. After passing under the second bridge, turn left along a tarmac track. Look right to see a labyrinth in the grass on the right of the track, with the 14th- and 15th-century church beyond. Go through the gate and turn right down the track, retracing your steps back to the start.

> **– To shorten**
>
> After descending Sourton Tors, at the cross-path junction just before the dip turn right down a path, keeping the steep-sided valley on your left. On nearing a wall bear right along a bridleway to Waypoint 2 and turn left back to the start. This reduces the walk by 1.5km (35min).

WALK 2
Meldon Reservoir

Start/finish	Meldon Reservoir
Locate	///digestion.hook.hiding
Cafes/pubs	None on route
Transport	No public transport
Parking	Meldon Reservoir pay-and-display car park (EX20 4LU)
Toilets	At car park

After crossing the 200m-long dam this walk follows a path along the length of Meldon Reservoir before swinging left and heading up the West Okement valley to the magical Black-a-Tor Copse. A stiff climb up to Black Tor gives some great views along the valley. From here you follow a track down Longstone Hill, steeply for a time, arriving back at the reservoir and retracing your outward route back to the start.

Time 2¾hr
Distance 8km (5 miles)
Climb 315m

Walk alongside a reservoir, visit a beautiful oak wood and, after a steep climb, enjoy the views from Black Tor

The lichen- and moss-covered oak trees and boulders at Black-a-Tor Copse

The walk follows a path along the length of Meldon Reservoir

1 Exit the car park via the steps beside the toilets, go through the gate and turn left along the access road. Cross the dam, which was built in 1972 to form **Meldon Reservoir**, go through the gate and turn right. Follow the track for 300m, keeping beside the fence on your right, to a junction. Through the small gate in the fence on the right are some picnic tables.

2 Keep ahead at the junction, following the path alongside the fence on the right for slightly under 1.5km. On the way, the path crosses a footbridge in a side-valley before continuing with views over the reservoir. Near the head of the reservoir the path curves left and heads down to a path junction and footbridge at **Vellake Corner**.

3 Keep left (do not cross the footbridge) and follow the path along the base of the steep slope of **Homerton Hill**, which rises up to your left with a small stream on your right. Then keep ahead up the valley, following the track, with the West Okement River on the right, to reach a gate and walled enclosure.

4 Follow a path passing to the left of the walled enclosure and continue alongside the West Okement River towards **Black-a-Tor Copse**. The onward route turns left shortly before

WALK 2 – MELDON RESERVOIR

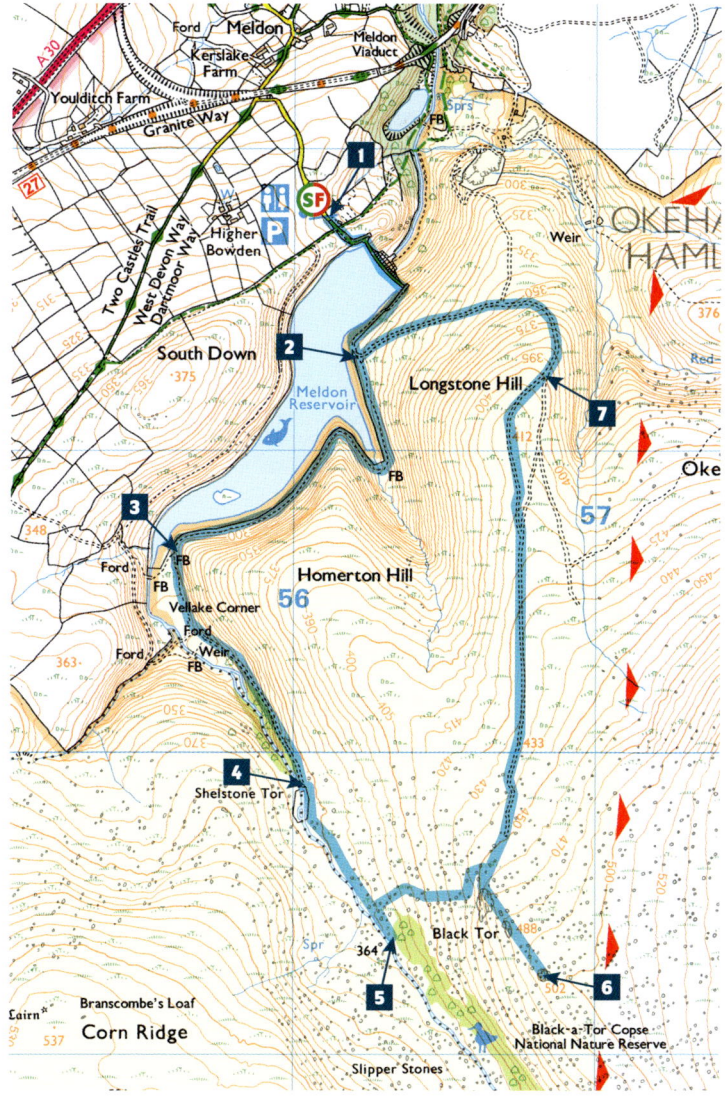

Following the track down Longstone Hill with views of the Red-a-ven Brook valley and West Mill Tor over to the right

the trees, but before that keep ahead to visit the copse.

Black-a-Tor Copse National Nature Reserve is home to ancient stunted English oaks growing amongst granite boulders clothed in moss and lichen. This is one of three high-altitude oak woods in Dartmoor, the others being Wistman's Wood and Piles Copse.

5 From the copse retrace your steps for 120m, then turn right and pick your way up the steep, boulder-strewn slope, keeping to the left of the outcrop. Then bear right to the first (lower) outcrop of **Black Tor**. The onward route turns left (north), but before that continue uphill to visit the other two outcrops that form Black Tor (502m). All three outcrops offer a great views over the West Okement valley.

6 Retrace your steps to the lower outcrop and bear half-right. At first the path is rather indistinct, but after 150m the route becomes easier to follow. The stony path crosses several wet areas as it gradually heads downhill. Continue along the grassy track over **Longstone Hill** to reach a track junction.

7 Keep left at the junction heading downhill. To your right is a view along the Red-a-ven Brook valley with (left to right), Rowtor, West Mill Tor and Yes Tor; ahead you can see Meldon Viaduct. Follow the track as it

WALK 2 – MELDON RESERVOIR

continues to curve left and descends more steeply towards the **reservoir**. On reaching the junction passed earlier, with a small gate opposite (Waypoint 2), turn right. Now retrace your outward route alongside the fence with the reservoir on your left and cross the dam back to the car park.

> **– To shorten**
>
> For a shorter walk follow the route to Vellake Corner (Waypoint 3) and then retrace your steps. This reduces the walk by 4km (1hr 15min) and saves 150m climbing.

Black Tor looking north from the middle outcrop to the first outcrop and beyond

Heading down Longstone Hill back to Meldon Reservoir

The summit of High Willhays – the highest point in Dartmoor and southern England

WALK 3
High Willhays and Yes Tor

CHALLENGE ROUTE

Time 3½hr
Distance 10.5km (6½ miles)
Climb 275m

Choose a nice day for this high-level challenging walk to enjoy the views from Dartmoor's highest summits

Start/finish	*Rowtor car park*
Locate	*///trappings.puffed.paint*
Cafes/pubs	*None on route*
Transport	*No public transport*
Parking	*Rowtor car park (EX20 1QR) near Okehampton Camp*
Toilets	*No public toilets on route*

Most of the walking on this route is along military tracks with steady gradients – however, there are two streams to cross with no footbridges. This is a high-level walk that visits Dartmoor's two highest summits, so be prepared with appropriate clothing, and don't attempt the walk in bad weather or low visibility. This walk lies within the Okehampton Military Range and can only be undertaken when the range is open.

Following the track up towards Yes Tor (right) and High Willhays (left)

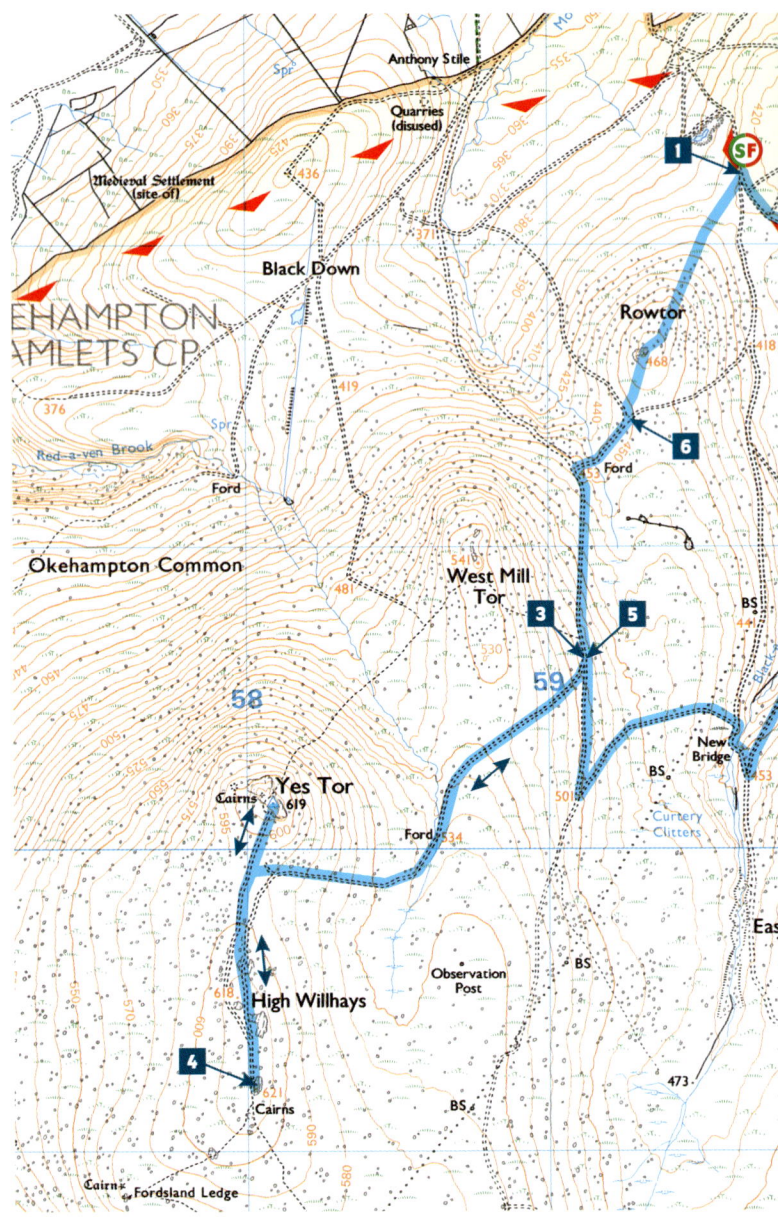

WALK 3 – HIGH WILLHAYS AND YES TOR

1 At the Y-junction beside the car park, fork left. Follow the tarmac military road for slightly under 1.5km, ignoring two tracks on the left and crossing the bridge over the **Black-a-ven Brook** to reach a military Observation Post (OP22), just after passing Hart Tor (436m) on the left.

2 Keep ahead down the track for 300m to a junction on the right. Turn right up the track, with **East Mill Tor** up to your left. At the next track junction, turn sharp right and shortly cross the Black-a-ven Brook at **New Bridge**. Continue for 75m to a track junction and turn left up to another track junction. Turn sharp right along the level track for 400m to a track junction and turn sharp left. For the shorter walk, or in bad weather, go straight on.

The Military Observation Post (OP22) near Hart Tor

3 Head up the track for 800m and cross the Red-a-ven Brook at a **ford** (there is no footbridge). Continue up the track more steeply to the ridge and a path junction. Turn right for 225m to the summit of **Yes Tor** (619m) with its trig point and military flagpole. Then retrace your steps and go straight on (southwards) passing two outcrops to a third one with a stone cairn – this is the summit of **High Willhays** (621m).

> High Willhays is both the highest point in Dartmoor and the highest point in southern England. Yes Tor comes a close second at just 2m lower. Both offer great views on a clear day.

4 Retrace your steps back towards **Yes Tor** and then turn right at the junction to retrace the outward route back down the track. Re-cross the Red-a-ven Brook and continue down to a junction (Waypoint 3).

5 Turn left down the track – with **West Mill Tor** on the left – to reach a junction. To the right are the remains of the Rowtor Target Railway that was built in 1959. Turn right and shortly cross a stream at a **ford** (no footbridge). Continue along the track to a Y-junction. For an easier route back, fork right down the track, later keeping left back to the car park.

6 To continue the walk fork left for 20m, then continue on a path up to **Rowtor** (468m). Although lower than its neighbours, Rowtor has a number of granite outcrops to explore and

Red-a-ven Brook ford looking towards West Mill Tor

The summit of Yes Tor is crowned by a trig point and military flagpole

some nice views. Continue in the same direction and follow a path downhill, keeping right at a Y-junction back to the car park, which is visible ahead.

> **– To shorten**
>
> At Waypoint 3 keep ahead to continue the walk, missing out Yes Tor and High Willhays. This reduces the walk by 5km (90min) and saves 130m climbing.

Okehampton Military Range

Since the early 1800s parts of Dartmoor have been used for military training by UK forces. From musket practice to munitions testing, and from navigation to survival and tactical training, Dartmoor has helped the armed services hone their skills. On North Dartmoor there are three live firing ranges marked with red and white posts: Okehampton, Merrivale and Willsworthy.

The public has access to these areas, except when live firing exercises are in progress. If the warning signals are displayed – red flags by day and red lamps by night – you must not enter the range. Check www.gov.uk/government/publications/dartmoor-firing-programme or phone 0800 458 4868.

The East Okement River near Cullever Steps

WALK 4
Cullever Steps

Start/finish	Okehampton railway station
Locate	///valuables.vipers.digs
Cafes/pubs	Cafe at railway station and cafe near youth hostel
Transport	Train and bus links to Okehampton
Parking	At railway station (EX20 1EJ)
Toilets	At railway station

Time 3hr
Distance 9.5km (6 miles)
Climb 295m

A longer route offering woodland and riverside walking, and tracks over the open moor with views of the East Okement valley

From the railway station follow the Devonshire Heartland Way before heading under the railway viaduct and road bridge. You then make a long steady climb along the East Okement River valley – which is rocky and steep at times – following the Dartmoor Way and Tarka Trail. From Cullever Steps the easier return route follows tracks, later heading down to Lower Halstock and skirting round East Hill before continuing down to the station.

The final leg of the walk heading back to Okehampton

SHORT WALKS DARTMOOR NORTH

Devonshire Heartland Way passing through meadows

1 Exit the **station** and turn left to a cross-junction. Turn right for a few paces, then turn sharp right along a tarmac track, signed Tramlines Bridleway and **Devonshire Heartland Way**. After the last house, go through a gate and follow the track through Tramlines Wood. Go through another gate and continue through the field, later following the track to the right (house on the left). Go through a gate and under the **railway viaduct**. The Dartmoor Way and Tarka Trail join from left and the walk now follows these two routes for 3km. Go through a gate and continue under the **road bridge** (A30) to a signed junction.

2 Keep ahead up the wooded valley with the **East Okement River** on your left; the route is rocky in places. Turn left to cross a footbridge over a side stream, go through a wall gap and continue up the East Okement valley, with a short steep section on the way. Continue up to a signed junction and turn left. For the shorter walk turn right.

The footbridge across the East Okement River shortly after Waypoint 3

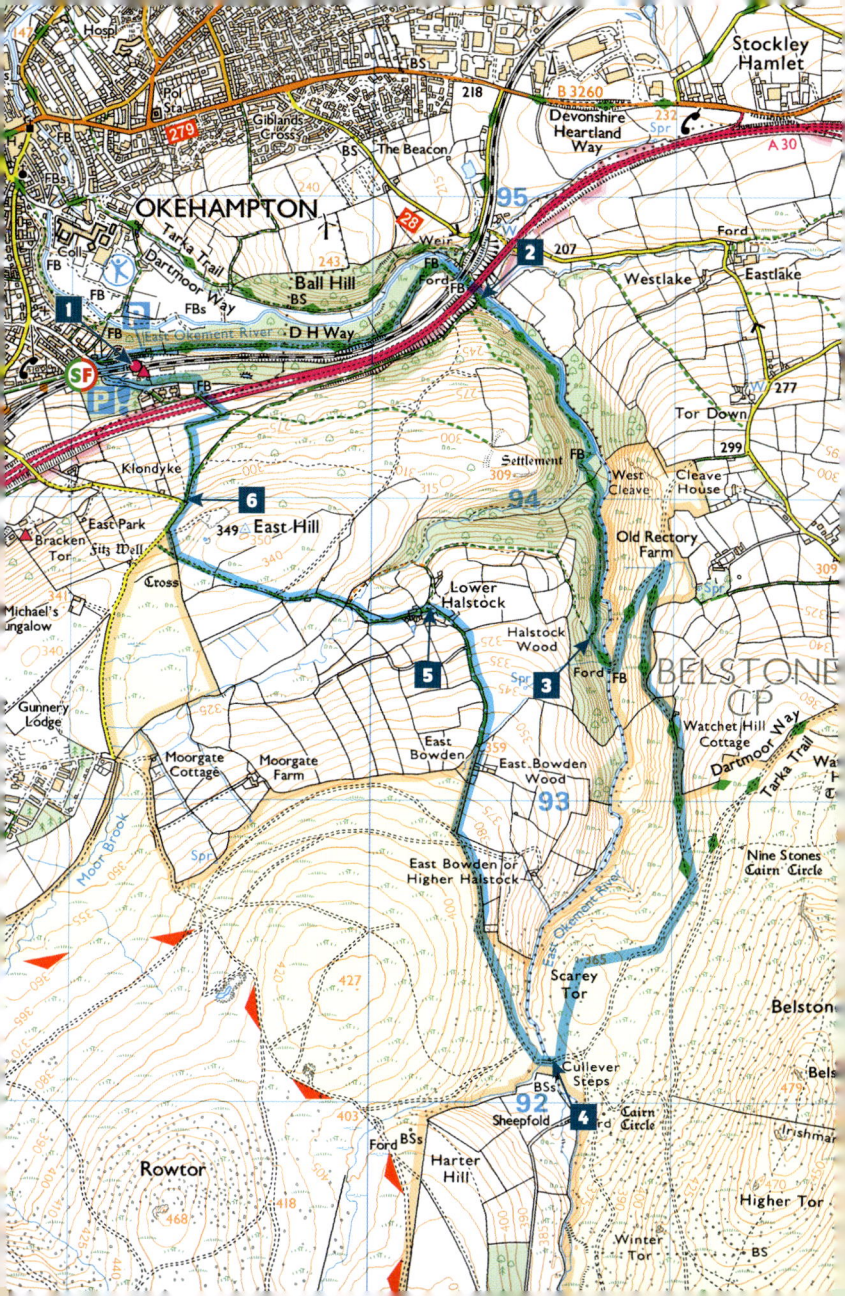

Passing the barn at East Bowden on the way down to Lower Halstock

3 Head downhill, cross the footbridge over the river and turn left up a path (not the steep path straight ahead). Turn sharp right along the track for slightly over 1km to a junction; the route gets narrower towards the end. Turn right along the track to a left-hand bend and fork right (straight on) along a path to **Scarey Tor** (365m). The tor, which makes a good picnic spot, offers views along the East Okement valley. Then turn left down a path to reach a track.

4 Turn right and cross the bridges over the East Okement River and Black-a-ven Brook at **Cullever Steps**.

> Cullever Steps consists of an old paved ford and a set of stepping stones across the East Okement River just upstream from the modern bridge. A short way downstream (right of the junction) is Cullever Steps Pool, a popular picnic and swimming spot.

Follow the track as it swings right to a junction and keep right (straight on) uphill. Continue up to a four-way junction, keep ahead for 50m to another junction and bear right alongside a stone wall (right). Go through the gate at the corner. Pass the barn at **East Bowden**, continue down the track (bridleway) to a signed three-way

junction at **Lower Halstock**. The shorter walk rejoins here.

5 Turn left and follow the tarmac track past farm buildings, cross a bridge and continue uphill, passing to the left of **East Hill**. Pass a cattle grid, turn right and then right down the road to the left-hand bend, where there are two side-by-side gates ahead.

6 Go through the left-hand gate, with a line of boundary trees on your right. Continue down to the bottom edge and turn right to a junction. Turn left through a gate, cross the footbridge over the A30 and go through another gate to a three-way junction (the right of way turns left). Keep ahead along the permitted path to Okehampton, down to a T-junction. Turn left and shortly exit the woodland through a gate. Turn right down the lane. The entrance on the right leads to the Granite Way Cafe (40m) and youth hostel. Pass under the railway bridge and turn right to the **railway station**.

> **– To shorten**
>
> At Waypoint 3 turn right uphill, follow the signed path to a three-way junction at Lower Halstock (Waypoint 5) and turn right to continue the walk. This reduces the walk by 3.5km (1hr) and saves 100m climbing.

The view from Belstone Tor looking north to Belstone Common Tor

WALK 5
Belstone and Belstone Common

Time 2hr
Distance 6.5km (4 miles)
Climb 205m

A picturesque village, a stiff climb up to some tors with lovely views, and an ancient stone cairn circle

Start/finish	Village green, Belstone
Locate	///leaves.shortens.friction
Cafes/pubs	Pub and tea room at Belstone
Transport	Buses from Exeter, Okehampton and Newton Abbot stop on the B3260 (Tongue End Cross) 1km north of Belstone
Parking	Belstone village car park (EX20 1RD)
Toilets	No public toilets on route

From Belstone follow a track along the River Taw valley before making a steep climb up to the ridge. Here the route turns right, taking you up past Higher Tor to Belstone Tor. After admiring the views, you pass the outcrops on Belstone Common before heading down the rock-strewn slope to the Nine Stones cairn circle. From here it's an easier walk along tracks and lanes back to Belstone. A shorter walk missing out the climb to Belstone Tor is also possible.

Following the Dartmoor Way and Tarka Trail back down towards Belstone

SHORT WALKS DARTMOOR NORTH

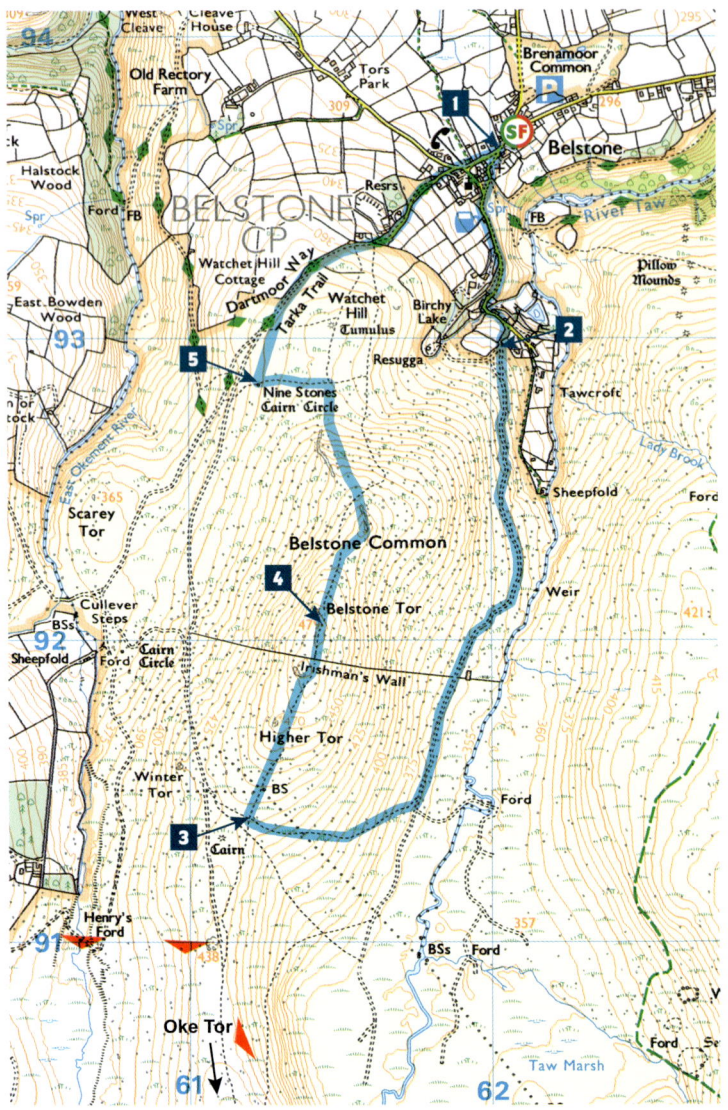

WALK 5 – BELSTONE AND BELSTONE COMMON

The former school in Belstone, now a tea room

1 Facing the Jubilee Stone on the village green in **Belstone**, fork left along the left-hand side of the green, with the Old School (now a tea room) on the left, and turn left at the junction; to the right is The Tors pub. Follow the lane for 500m to a Y-junction, shortly after curving left past some houses. Fork right uphill, go through a gate onto the open moor and keep ahead. For the shorter walk turn right.

2 Follow the track along the valley for slightly over 1.5km. Just before a track junction on the left, fork right up a path. Keep right at the Y-junction up to the ridge. To the left along the ridge is Oke Tor.

3 Turn right and head uphill, passing a large boulder, to **Higher Tor** (466m). There are views behind you (south) to Oke Tor and Steeperton Tor, with Taw Marsh to the left in the valley and High Willhays, Yes Tor and West Mill Tor to the right. Continue uphill past an outcrop, then cross **Irishman's Wall** – an east-west stone wall built around 1820 – to **Belstone Tor** (479m), another great place to sit and admire the views.

Irishman's Wall and Belstone Tor

4 Head downhill, passing **Belstone Common Tor** (450m) and follow a path down through the clitter (stones), passing to the right of Tors End Tor (412m); ahead is a military flagpole on Watchet Hill. On reaching a path junction as the steep slope levels out, turn left along a wide grassy path to **Nine Stones**.

Nine Stones, also known as the Nine Maidens or 'dancing stones', is the remains of a Bronze Age burial cairn circle. Folklore has it that the stones are actually nine maidens cast into stone for dancing on the Sabbath.

5 From Nine Stones turn right and keep ahead at cross path junctions to join a track. Keep ahead, now following the **Dartmoor Way** and **Tarka Trail** with a wall on your left, heading downhill. Go through a gate and walk down the lane, keeping ahead at junctions to reach the village green in **Belstone**.

As you walk down the lane towards the village green, the first lane on the right leads to the 15th-century Church of St Mary the Virgin; inside is an early medieval Ring Cross carved on a granite slab. The second lane on the right leads to The Tors pub.

SHORT WALKS DARTMOOR NORTH

Nine Stones – the remains of a cairn circle

ⓘ *To the east of Belstone is Sticklepath and the 19th-century, water-powered Finch Foundry. In its heyday, the foundry made 400 tools a day, ranging from scythes to shovels (www.nationaltrust.org.uk/visit/devon/finch-foundry).*

ⓘ *The Tarka Trail is a 290km, figure-of-eight long-distance trail through North Devon, following in the footsteps of the otter in Henry Williamson's well-known novel,* **Tarka the Otter** *(1927).*

— To shorten

At Waypoint 2 turn right up a grassy track, keep left of the trees and cross a stream (no footbridge). Then bear left up a wide grassy path to Nine Stones (Waypoint 5) to continue the walk. This reduces the walk by 3.5km (1hr) and saves 100m climbing.

+ To lengthen

If the Okehampton Military Range is open (no red flag flying), from Waypoint 3 turn left along the ridge-top path to Oke Tor (466m), then retrace your steps. This adds 3km (1hr).

WALK 6
Kestor Rock and Scorhill Down

Start/finish	Scorhill car park, near Gidleigh
Locate	///reckons.dubbing.riots
Cafes/pubs	None on route
Transport	No public transport
Parking	Small car park at end of lane, near Gidleigh (TQ13 8HS)
Toilets	No public toilets on route

This walk follows lanes down to Gidleigh before heading through Gidleigh Wood. After crossing the North Teign River there is a short steep ascent before a more gradual climb along paths and lanes to Kestor Rock on Chagford Common. After you've soaked up the view, the route continues over open moor, passing some ancient stone rows and crossing the North Teign River. The final stop is the atmospheric Scorhill stone circle from where it is a short walk back to the car park.

Time 2¾hr
Distance 8.5km (5¼ miles)
Climb 275m

Visit a historic church, climb a tor with a view and explore some fascinating ancient sites

Holy Trinity Church at Gidleigh

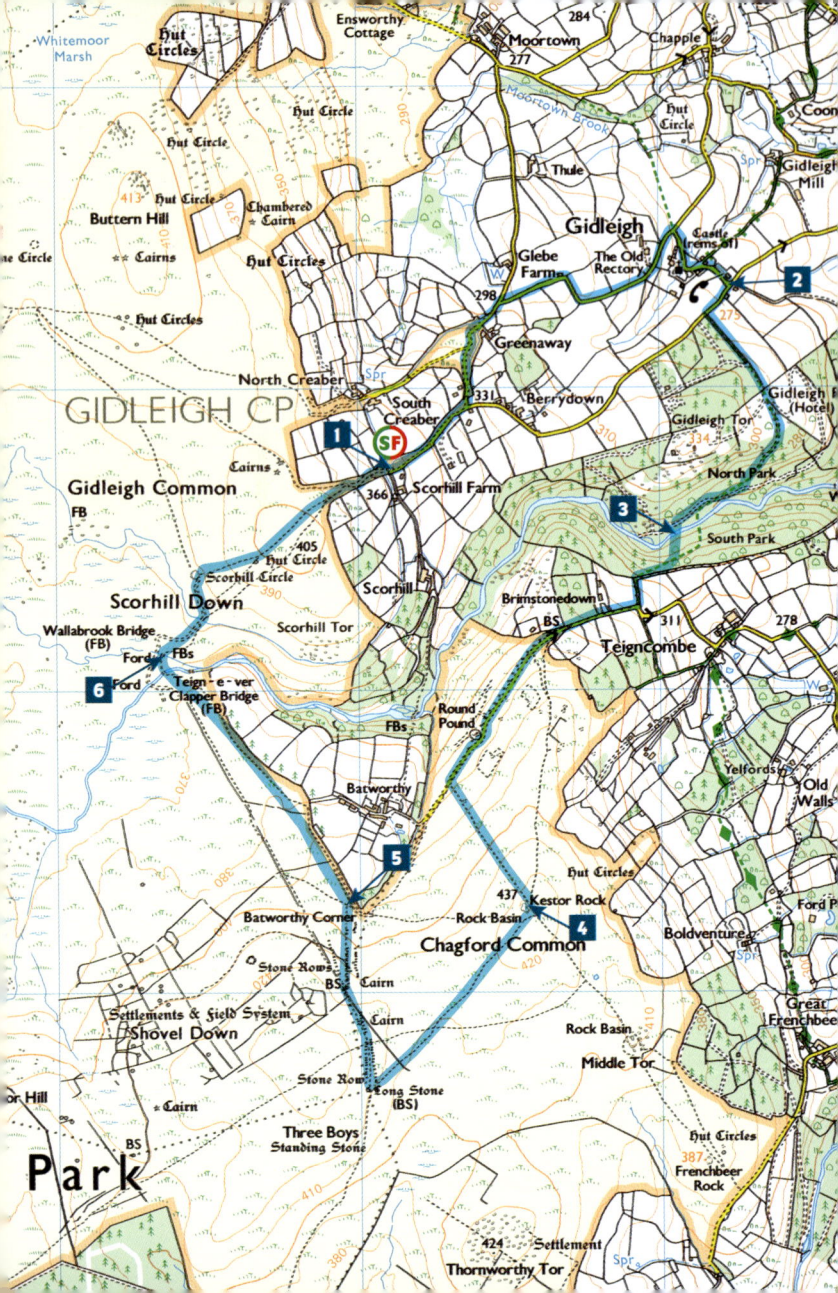

Rock basin on the top of Kestor Rock

1 From the car park near **Scorhill Farm** walk down the lane to a junction. Turn left down the lane, keeping right at the next three junctions, heading towards **Gidleigh** to reach the church on your right. Inside the late 15th-century Holy Trinity Church is a wonderful 16th-century roodscreen. Nearby (on private land) are the ruins of a 14th-century fortified manor house. Follow the lane to a T-junction (Gidleigh Cross) beside the village hall.

2 Turn right and head uphill for 125m, then turn left along a track. Pass a gate and keep ahead through Gidleigh Wood for 300m to a Y-junction. Follow the signed path straight on between the two tracks, heading down through the trees and passing below the outcrops of **Gidleigh Tor**. Turn right along the track for 250m to a footpath sign and turn left across the footbridge over the **North Teign River**.

3 Follow the path steeply uphill, crossing a track on the way to a track at the top. Turn right and then left following the track up past a gate. Turn right up the lane for 700m, passing a cattle grid to reach the **Round Pound** on your right. This circular enclosure, with the remains of a large, centrally placed hut, dates from the late Bronze and Iron Age. Continue along the lane for 150m, then turn left following a path up to **Kestor Rock** (437m). For a shorter walk keep ahead along the lane.

SHORT WALKS DARTMOOR NORTH

The prominent stack of Kestor Rock has an impressive rock basin. Views include Fernworthy Forest (south), Meldon Hill (east), Watern Tor (west) and the dome of Cosdon Beacon (north-west).

4 Take the second path on the right and head across fairly level ground for 800m to the **Long Stone** (visible from the tor) and turn right. Head along the path following a line of stones over the brow of the hill to reach a double stone row and continue alongside this. Soon there is another double stone row heading towards **Batworthy Corner** from the remains of the Fourfold Cairn Circle. Follow this stone row towards the trees and turn left.

The Long Stone, the first of several Bronze Age relics to be found

The Long Stone standing stone

on Shovel Down, is Dartmoor's fourth tallest menhir (3.1m). It was more recently used as a boundary marker between Chagford, Gidleigh and the Duchy of Cornwall land. Other remains include several stone rows (both double and single) and the Fourfold Cairn Circle.

Teign-e-ver Clapper Bridge

Scorhill stone circle looking towards Watern Tor

5 Continue along the path running parallel to the trees and wall on your right. Keep ahead and cross the **Teigne-ver Clapper Bridge** over the North Teign River. Then cross a smaller clapper bridge over the Walla Brook.

To visit the Tolmen Stone – a large boulder with a circular hole – turn right alongside the Walla Brook for 125m to a point soon after it joins the North Teign River; then retrace your steps.

ⓘ *Clapper bridges consist of flat slabs of granite supported on stone pillars for wider streams and rivers, or single slabs resting on the banks of smaller streams. The name 'clapper' is probably from the Anglo-Saxon* cleaca *meaning 'stepping stone'.*

6 Bear half-right and soon cross a third bridge over the Gallavan Brook and bear half-left to the **Scorhill Circle**. Atmospheric (and unrestored) Scorhill Circle dates from the Bronze Age. The onward route turns right uphill. Continue over the brow of the hill, then down between walls and through the gate back to the parking area.

– To shorten

From Round Pound keep ahead along the lane and path to Batsworthy Corner and turn right to continue the walk. This reduces the walk by 1.5km (30min).

The Market House – or 'Pepperpot' – in The Square at Chagford

WALK 7
Chagford and Meldon Hill

Time 1¾hr
Distance 5km (3 miles)
Climb 230m

Explore a lively town and make a steep ascent and descent of a tor for a great view

Start/finish	The Square, Chagford
Locate	///steady.haggis.cheeses
Cafes/pubs	Pubs and cafes in Chagford
Transport	Buses from Moretonhampstead, Okehampton, Newton Abbot and Exeter stop at Chagford
Parking	Car park in Chagford (TQ13 8DP)
Toilets	In The Square, Chagford

From Chagford the route follows lanes to the edge of the town. Then the going gets a bit more strenuous as you follow lanes up past Meldon Hall before a final climb up a grassy path brings you to the top of Meldon Hill. After soaking up the views head downhill, steeply at times, before crossing Padley Common on the way back to The Square. A shorter, more level walk is also possible.

Heading down to Padley Common

SHORT WALKS DARTMOOR NORTH

Church of St Michael the Archangel at Chagford

1 From The Square in **Chagford** stand facing the Ring O' Bells pub with the Market House – also known as the 'Pepperpot' – behind you and turn left along the High Street. Pass the Three Crowns (right), the church (left) and the Globe Inn (right) to come to a junction, then turn right along New Street (left leads to the main car park). Continue along Meldon Road to the edge of the town and pass a cattle grid to some granite posts on the right. The shorter walk goes right here.

2 With care, continue up the lane, passing **Meldon Hall** (right) to reach a junction. Turn right up the lane for 350m and turn right over a stile. Head diagonally left up through the field, cross a stile on the right a short way from the field corner and continue across the corner of the next field. Leave over another stile and turn right up the lane for 400m to a building and track junction on the left.

WALK 7 – CHAGFORD AND MELDON HILL

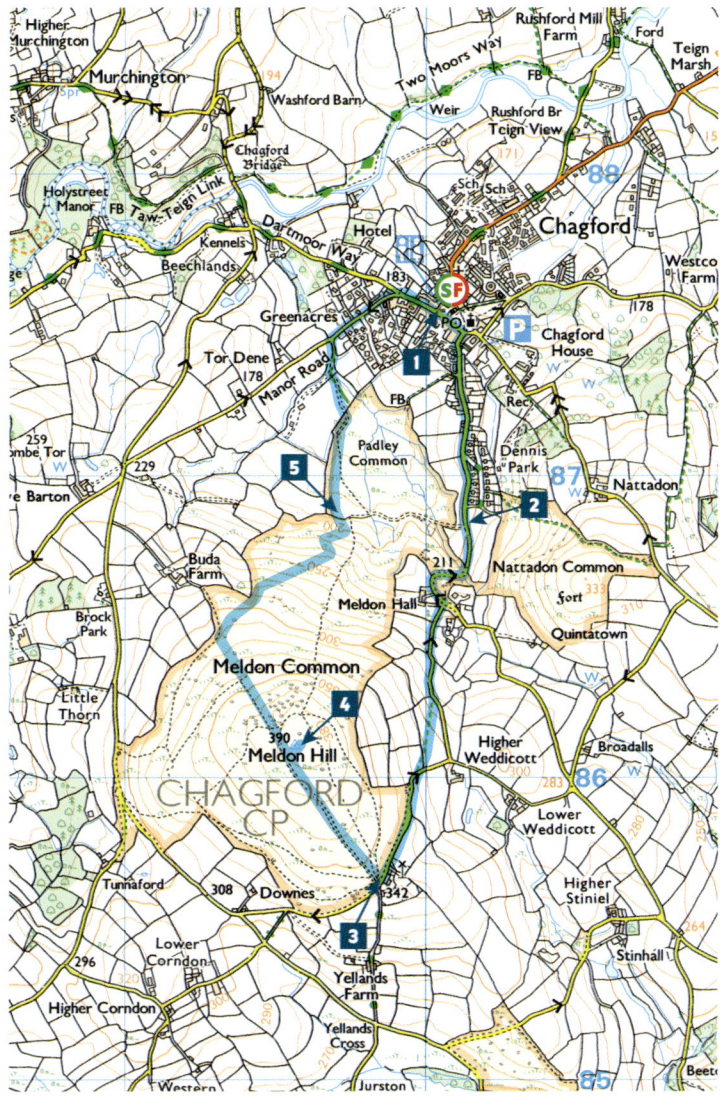

SHORT WALKS DARTMOOR NORTH

3 Turn right and follow the wide grassy path gradually climbing up **Meldon Hill** (390m). On nearing the top, turn right up to the trig point. Meldon Hill is crowned by several tors that are all worth exploring for their slightly different views.

ⓘ A large part of Dartmoor is made of granite that was created around 295 million years ago. Weathering and erosion formed the characteristic tors that can be seen today.

From the trig point the view includes Cosdon Hill (north-west), Castle Drogo (north-east), Haytor Rocks (south-east), Fernworthy Forest (south-west) and Kestor Rock (west), with Watern Tor in the distance. On the northern tor there is also a good example of a rock basin.

4 After exploring the other outcrops, head back to the trig point and retrace your steps back to the main path and turn right. Keep ahead, passing

The summit of Meldon Hill

between an outcrop on the left and one over to the right. Head downhill to a path junction with a boundary ahead and turn right. Follow the narrow path as it descends **Meldon Common**. Later the path gets a bit steeper as it zigzags downhill to the bottom of the slope beside a metal seat. The shorter walk joins from the right.

5 Keep ahead along the left-hand side of **Padley Common** to a gate on the left, just after passing the cricket ground (left). Turn left through the gate and shortly go through another gate. Bear right along the concrete track to a road and turn right up to a junction. Turn right up along Mill Street back to The Square in **Chagford**.

> **— To shorten**
>
> At Waypoint 2 turn right down past the granite posts, keep ahead over a footbridge to the open common, pass two metal seats and turn right to rejoin the main walk at Waypoint 5. This reduces the walk by 2.5km (1hr) and saves 175m climbing.

Chagford

Chagford is a former 'Stannary Town' where smelted tin was brought for assaying and taxation. In The Square is the unusual octagonal Market House built in 1862, known locally as the 'Pepperpot'. The 15th-century Church of St Michael the Archangel is also worth a visit. Take a look at the roof bosses which include the 'tinners' rabbits' – each rabbit has two ears, but there are only three ears between them. The town has a range of facilities, including cafes, pubs and independent shops.

'Tinners' rabbits' roof boss inside the church at Chagford

Following a path alongside Fernworthy Reservoir

WALK 8
Fernworthy Reservoir

Start/finish	*Fernworthy Reservoir*
Locate	*///adjuster.plugs.halt*
Cafes/pubs	*None on route*
Transport	*No public transport*
Parking	*Fernworthy Reservoir pay-and-display car park (TQ13 8EF)*
Toilets	*At car park*

Time 2½hr
Distance 7.5km (4¾ miles)
Climb 200m

Fairly easy walking on paths and forestry tracks skirting round a reservoir and visiting some ancient sites

From the car park this walk follows paths near to the reservoir for a while before making a loop up through Fernworthy Forest, visiting an ancient stone circle on the way. The route then continues alongside the reservoir, passing an impressive cist before zigzagging below the dam to cross the river. The final leg heads back up to the dam before continuing alongside the water back to the car park.

A frosty start at Fernworthy Reservoir

SHORT WALKS DARTMOOR NORTH

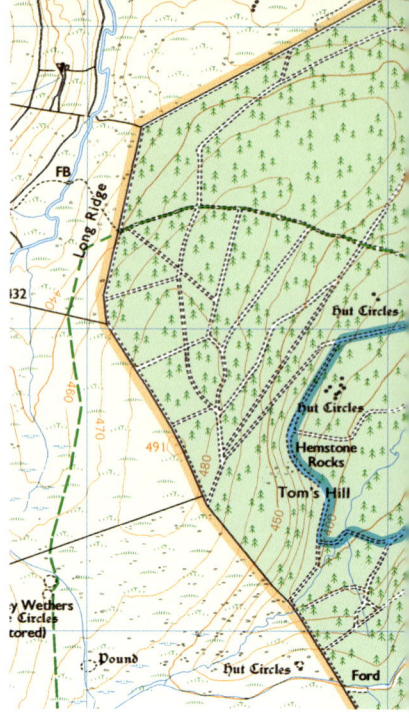

1 Head towards the **car park** entrance and bear right in front of the building (toilet and information boards) to a track. Turn right down the track for 250m with **Fernworthy Reservoir** a short way off to the right. The reservoir was built in 1942 to supply water for the Torquay area. Bear left through a small gate and continue along the gravel path. Keep ahead through trees, cross a footbridge and follow the path as it curves right and then left to pass just left of a bird hide. Go through a gate, keep ahead to a lane opposite a large barn.

2 Turn right along the lane and after crossing **Sandeman Bridge**, turn left onto a forestry track. For a shorter walk keep ahead along the lane. Pass the vehicle barrier and keep ahead (right) at the track junction through **Fernworthy Forest**. This is the largest plantation on Dartmoor and was planted in the 1920s to replenish timber supplies following WW1. The track later curves left and crosses a bridge over a stream before heading up to a track junction.

3 Turn right, then fork right at the Y-junction heading downhill and cross a bridge over a stream. Continue up to a T-junction and turn right. Follow the track uphill and then downhill to a cross-track junction. Shortly after starting to descend, you can find the remains of a hut circle 20m left of the track.

4 Turn right for 100m, then turn left past two large boulders and continue to the **Fernworthy Circle** – beyond it is a double stone row and to the right is a burial cairn.

> **The stone circle (also known as the Froggymead Stone Circle), which consists of 27 stones, and the adjacent double stone row and burial cairn date from the late Neolithic and early Bronze Age.**

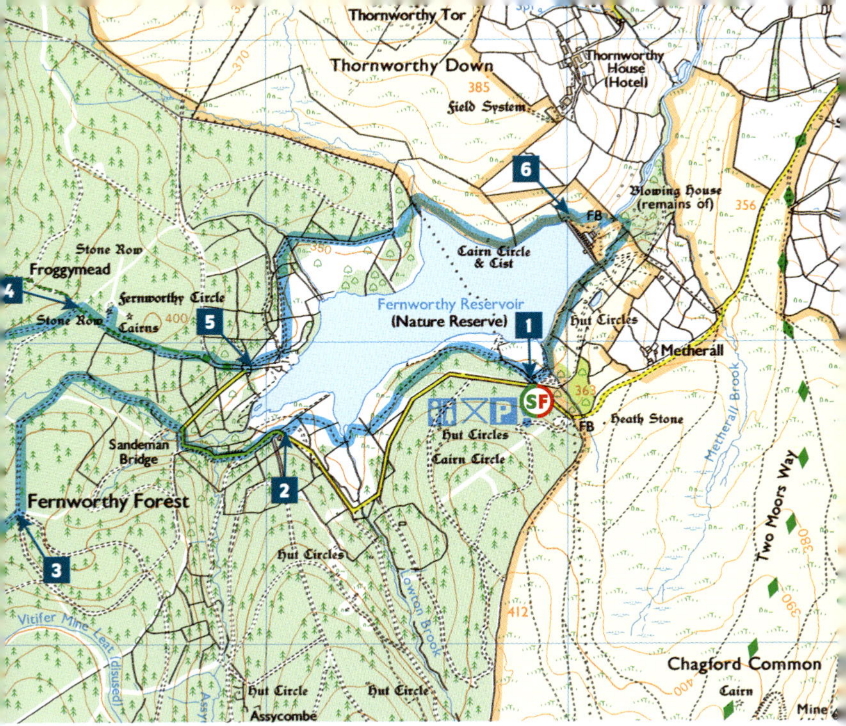

Fernworthy stone circle

Retrace your steps back to the track, turn left downhill and later go through a gate to a junction with the end of a lane. The shorter walk rejoins here.

5 Turn left, then go through a small gate and follow the reservoir path in a clockwise direction, keeping ahead through more gates. Continue along the path, through a wet area, as it curves to the right. Continue through gates and shortly cross a footbridge over a stream. The path now stays close to the water's edge, passing a **cist** a few metres to the left of the path, to reach the dam. The Thornworthy Cist is the remains of a late Neolithic or early Bronze Age burial chamber.

6 Immediately after passing the end of the dam, bear right and go through a gate. Follow the zigzag path downhill and cross a footbridge over the **South**

The dam at Fernworthy Reservoir

The Thornworthy Cist

Teign River. Bear left uphill, then right along the track for a short distance before forking left up a path. Turn right along the tarmac track towards the dam and go through a gate. Continue with the reservoir on your right to an open area with picnic tables and turn left up to the car park.

> **– To shorten**
>
> After Sandeman Bridge continue along the lane to rejoin the main walk at Waypoint 5. This reduces the walk by 3km (1hr) and saves 110m of climbing.

The Hunter's Path towards Sharp Tor

WALK 9
River Teign

Start/finish	Fingle Bridge
Locate	///blip.superhero.hamster
Cafes/pubs	Pub at Fingle Bridge, cafe at Castle Drogo
Transport	Buses from Exeter to Chagford and Moretonhamstead stop at Castle Drogo Drive (700m off route)
Parking	Roadside parking along lane, or National Trust car park across the bridge (EX6 6PW)
Toilets	In car park at Fingle Bridge (100m off route) and Castle Drogo (400m off route)

Time 2hr
Distance 6.5km (4 miles)
Climb 240m

A walk along the picturesque wooded Teign Valley from Fingle Bridge, with an option to visit an interesting castle

From Fingle Bridge set out along the Dartmoor Way with a steep climb up through Drewston Wood. The walking becomes easier as you follow the Hunter's Path past Sharp Tor, with views across the wooded Teign Valley, passing below Castle Drogo. After Hunter's Tor the route heads downhill to cross the River Teign before following the river along the wooded valley back to Fingle Bridge. There is an option to visit the impressive Castle Drogo, England's last castle.

Following the track along the wooded valley back to Fingle Bridge

The Fingle Bridge Inn

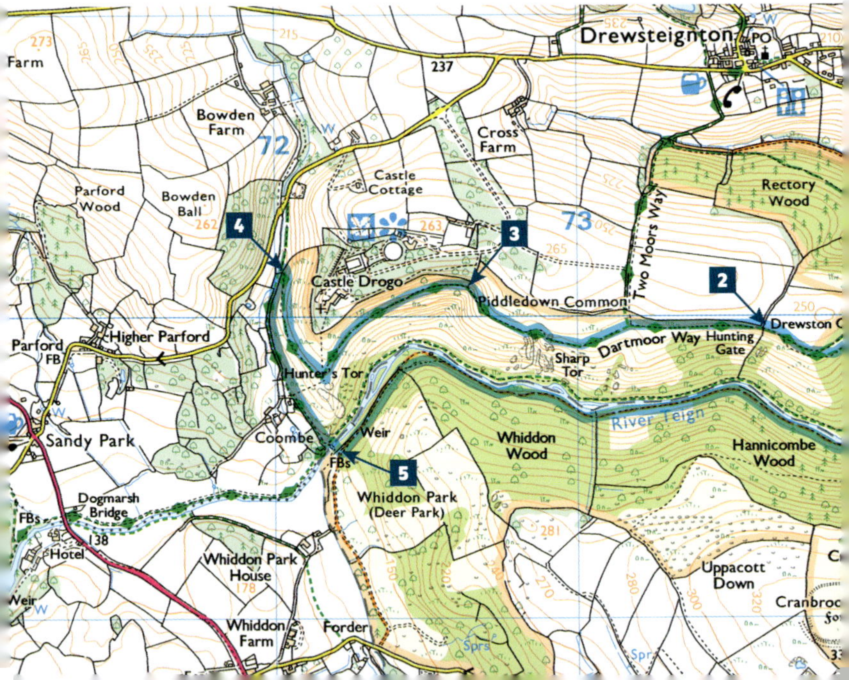

WALK 9 – RIVER TEIGN

1 From the north side of **Fingle Bridge**, with the Fingle Bridge Inn over to your right, walk along the lane heading away from the river. The bridge, which crosses the River Teign, is a fine example of a 17th-century three-arched packhorse bridge. After 140m (parking on right) turn sharp left and follow the bridleway (**Dartmoor Way**) steeply up though Drewston Wood to a junction. Turn left along the Hunter's Path and shortly go through the **Hunting Gate**.

2 Continue along the Hunter's Path – on the way the Two Moors Way joins from the right – to a signed junction at **Sharp Tor**. Take a break and enjoy the views over the Teign Valley, but be careful, it's a steep drop. Follow the Hunter's Path for 300m to another signed junction and keep ahead. To visit Castle Drogo (National Trust, entrance fee applies) turn right here.

3 Follow the Hunter's Path downhill, with **Castle Drogo** up to the right, to a junction near **Hunter's Tor** and turn right. Continue down the path, with the castle up to your right, and go through gates to a surfaced track.

4 Turn left down the surfaced track (signed for Fisherman's Path and River Teign), then fork left along a track (signed for Gibhouse and footpath). Shortly before the cottage (Gibhouse), fork left along a narrower path down to a junction. Turn left, then immediately turn right across the **footbridge** (also known as Iron Bridge) over the River Teign. Keep ahead and cross the wall via the stone steps.

> ⓘ *Not far from Drewsteignton is Stone Lane Gardens, an attractive woodland and water garden dotted with sculptures, known for its National Collections of birch and alder trees (www.stonelanegardens.com).*

SHORT WALKS DARTMOOR NORTH

> ⓘ *The Dartmoor Way, a 173km long circular route around Dartmoor, visits many of the towns and villages that nestle on the edge of Dartmoor.*

5 Turn left along the track, keeping the high granite wall that once formed the boundary of **Whiddon Deer Park** on your left. Go through a gate where the route splits and follow the right-hand fork (track) uphill. The left-hand fork passes the Hydro Turbine building that was built to generate electricity for the castle. Continue along the track through **Whiddon Wood** and **Hannicombe Wood** following the River Teign downstream to a track junction. Some 100m to the right is the National Trust car park and toilets. Turn left across **Fingle Bridge** back to the start.

> ⓘ *Drewsteignton is home to the thatched, community-owned Drewe Arms; the pub was run by Mabel Mudge and her husband for 75 years until she retired in 1994 at the grand age of 99.*

Following the high stone wall that once formed the edge of the deer park

Castle Drogo

Castle Drogo

The early 20th-century Castle Drogo – said to be the last castle built in England – was designed and built by Sir Edwin Lutyens for Julius Drewe, founder of the Home and Colonial Stores which, in the 1920s, was one of the UK's largest retail chains. Drewe chose the site as he believed, mistakenly, that his ancestors had connections with the nearby village of Drewsteignton. The formal gardens, also designed by Lutyens, are noted for their rhododendrons, magnolias and roses. The castle and grounds were given to the National Trust in 1974 (www.nationaltrust.org.uk/visit/devon/castle-drogo).

+ To lengthen

To visit Castle Drogo at Waypoint 3 turn right up the steps, go through a gate and continue uphill. Go through another gate, continue up to a tarmac drive and turn left following the signs to the castle and shop. Retrace your steps back down to Waypoint 3 and turn right to continue the walk. This adds 400m each way plus time for visiting the castle and gardens.

Path through woods between Tottiford Reservoir and Trenchford Reservoir

WALK 10
Three Reservoirs

Start/finish	Trenchford Reservoir
Locate	///defected.advising.boomers
Cafes/pubs	None on route
Transport	No public transport
Parking	Trenchford Reservoir pay-and-display car park (TQ13 9NZ), accessed off A382 at Slade Cross
Toilets	At car park

Time 2hr
Distance 6km (3¾ miles)
Climb 120m

Easy walking along paths, tracks and lanes through woodland and alongside peaceful reservoirs

This reasonably level walk soon offers views over Trenchford Reservoir as you follow a lane across the dam. The walk then follows a tree-shaded shoreline path beside Tottiford Reservoir before heading through pine plantations, following a mix of lanes, tracks and paths. After a quick visit to Kennick Reservoir you continue through pine plantations to Trenchford Reservoir from where it's an easy walk back to the car park. A shorter walk is also possible.

Kennick Reservoir

Trenchford Reservoir

1 Head back towards the car park entrance at **Bullaton Cross** and turn left through the picnic area. Follow the path parallel with the lane which is on your right, soon with views to the left over **Trenchford Reservoir**. Go through a gate and turn left along the lane (crossing the dam on the way) to a three-way junction and fork right. For a shorter walk turn left.

2 Follow the track (private road) for 50m and then fork left to the water's edge. Continue along the path, which can be muddy in places, keeping **Tottiford Reservoir** on your left for 1km to a four-way junction.

3 Turn right and follow the path up through the trees, keeping straight on (right) at a path junction, and follow the path as it swings right and left. Go through a gate and turn left along the lane to a junction. Turn left (in the direction of Moretonhampstead) for 100m and then turn right along the track (bridleway). At the right-hand bend, turn left along a path (signed for Kennick Reservoir), and later keep ahead at a path junction and continue to join a lane.

4 Follow the lane to **Kennick Reservoir** (right). Ignore a signed path to the left (this can be muddy) and instead continue across the dam. As the lane curves right, turn left through a gate. The path splits – fork left down to a junction (footbridge to the left) and keep ahead for 100m to another three-way junction with the reservoir on your left.

5 Turn right up through the trees (in the direction of Trenchford). Keep ahead at a path junction and go through a gate to a lane. Turn left and immediately turn right through another gate. Follow the path to a T-junction. Turn left and follow the

The junction on the way to Kennick Reservoir

View of Trenchford Reservoir from the footbridge

path down through the trees to a three-way junction (with a footbridge ahead). Turn left to reach another three-way junction. The shorter walk rejoins here.

6 Turn right and cross the long **footbridge**. Turn left and follow the path with **Trenchford Reservoir** once more on your left. Later head slightly uphill following the tree-shaded path to the car park.

> **– To shorten**
>
> At Waypoint 2 turn left across the dam, then turn left through a gate. Follow the path with Trenchford Reservoir on your left to a three-way junction and turn left. Now continue the walk from Waypoint 6. This reduces the walk by 3km (50min) and saves 70m climbing.

The Reservoirs

The three adjacent reservoirs of Trenchford, Tottiford and Kennick were created to supply drinking water to the Torbay area of Devon. Tottiford, the oldest reservoir in Dartmoor, was built in 1861, followed by Kennick Reservoir in the early 1880s and then Trenchford Reservoir in the early 1900s. Well-used permitted footpaths encircle both Trenchford and Tottisford; Kennick Reservoir is reserved for angling. In the middle of Tottiford Reservoir, during very low water levels in 2009, an ancient late Neolithic and Bronze Age ceremonial complex was revealed. The site included stone rows, burial cairns and a stone circle.

WALK 11
Bovey Valley Woods and Lustleigh

Time 2½hr
Distance 8km (5 miles)
Climb 290m

A rollercoaster of a walk exploring wooded Lustleigh Cleave and visiting a picturesque village

Start/finish	*Pullabrook Wood, near Drakeford Bridge*
Locate	*///incursion.edits.work*
Cafes/pubs	*Pub and tea room at Lustleigh*
Transport	*Buses between Newton Abbot and Moretonhampstead stop at Lustleigh (300m off route)*
Parking	*Pullabrook car park, Bovey Valley Woods (TQ13 9SJ)*
Toilets	*At Lustleigh*

This undulating walk explores the lovely woods of the Bovey Valley. Start by following a track through Pullabrook Wood, then along the old Manaton road before crossing the River Bovey at Hisley Bridge. After a stiff climb through Hisley Wood head downhill to picturesque Lustleigh. The route then follows lanes and tracks up past Lower Hisley before a steep descent through Hisley Wood leads back to Hisley Bridge. The final section meanders alongside the River Bovey to Drakeford Bridge. A shorter walk out and back along the river is also possible.

The village green and cross at Lustleigh

Hisley Bridge over the River Bovey

1 From the back of the car park go through the gate and follow the track (Dartmoor Way) through **Pullabrook Wood**, keeping ahead along the main track at junctions.

> Pullabrook Wood, Hisley Wood and Houndtor Wood form the Woodland Trust's Bovey Valley Woods, a well-known location for birdwatching. They are part of the East Dartmoor National Nature Reserve, which provides a mosaic of important woodland, heathland and wetland habitats.

Leave the woods through a gate and turn right down the track (Old Manaton Road). At a track junction, after passing a large rounded boulder on your right, turn right to a gate.

Nearing the top of Hisley Wood

WALK 11 – BOVEY VALLEY WOODS AND LUSTLEIGH

2 Go through the gate, cross Hisley Bridge – a picturesque medieval packhorse bridge – over the River Bovey and fork left up to a junction. For the shorter walk turn right along the riverside path. Turn left, following the track up through **Hisley Wood** for 900m to a junction (where a permissive bridleway turns right). This steep-sided valley, known as Lustleigh Cleave, follows the line of the Sticklepath Fault that formed 65–50 million years ago.

3 Go straight on through a gate and follow the path steeply up to another

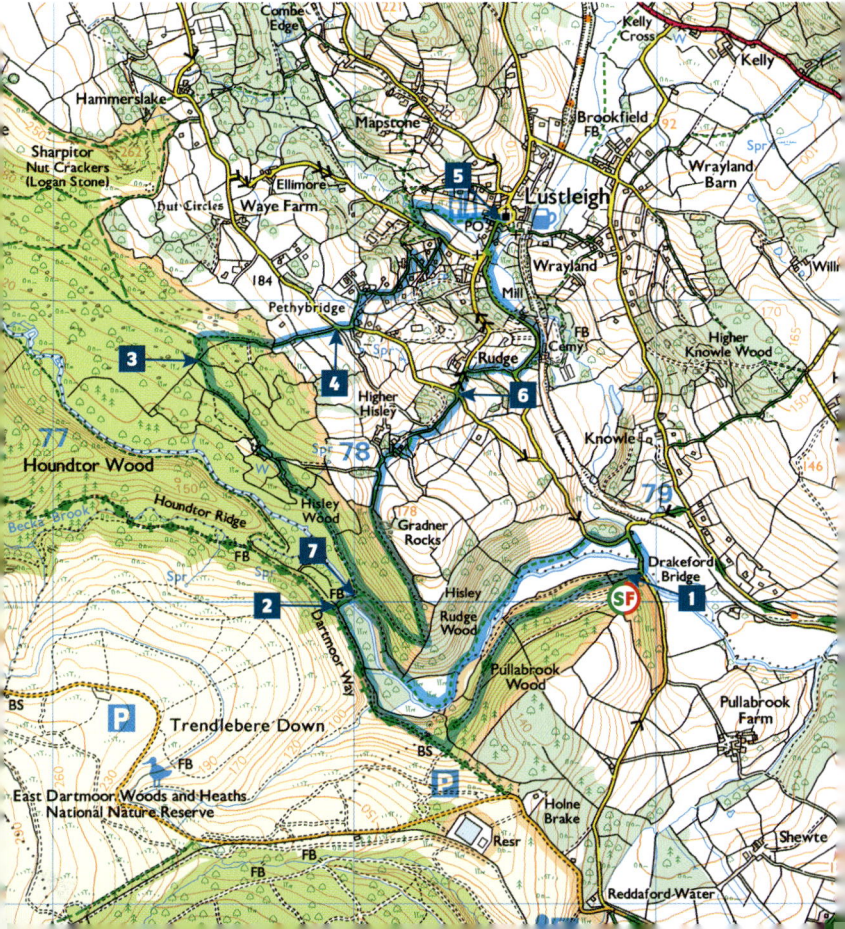

junction. Turn right up the bridleway (the permissive bridleway soon joins from the right) and go through a gate at the top. Follow the enclosed route down to a minor road.

4 Turn right along the road to a junction and turn left down the lane (**Pethybridge**). Keep right at the next junction and follow the lane for 450m down past thatched cottages to a T-junction. Turn left and shortly after passing a house on the right, turn right down a signed path. Keep right and go through a gate. Cross the footbridge and continue through open meadow (Town Orchard), aiming for the church tower in **Lustleigh**. Town Orchard is the location of the May Day festival, and the large boulder and seat is where the May Queen is crowned. Leave the meadow through a gate, follow the lane (toilets on the right) to a cross-junction beside the shop and turn right.

> Straight across the junction is the tea room, village green, Cleave pub and the 13th-century Church of St John the Baptist. Inside the church is Datuidoc's Stone, a 6th-century sculptured gravestone.

5 Follow the road down to a junction. Fork left along Mill Lane for 650m to a left-hand bend shortly after passing an entrance on the left. Turn right

Thatched cottage at Pethybridge

The May Queen stone and seat at Lustleigh

> ⓘ *The historic estate of Parke near Bovey Tracey has way-marked woodland and riverside trails beside the River Bovey, a walled garden, orchard and cafe (www.nationaltrust.org.uk/visit/devon/parke).*

up the bridleway, then left up the road to a junction at **Rudge**.

6 Follow the track opposite (signed for Lower Hisley) uphill. Later fork left to continue along the enclosed bridleway. Go through a small gate and bear right then left past the farm buildings. Pass through another gate and shortly follow the track steeply down through **Hisley Wood** to a junction. Turn left to a junction just before Hisley Bridge.

7 Turn left along the riverside path (with the river on your right). Go through a gate and continue (keeping the river over to the right), passing **Rudge Wood** and an open meadow. Go through a gate and continue through the field, leave through another gate and turn right along the lane to a T-junction. Turn right and after crossing **Drakeford Bridge** turn right back to the car park.

— To shorten

Immediately after crossing Hisley Bridge turn right at Waypoint 7 and follow the riverside path (river on right). This reduces the walk by 4.5km (1hr 30min) and saves 190m climbing.

Path leading up to Hookney Tor

WALK 12
Grimspound and Bennett's Cross

Start/finish Warren House Inn on B3212
Locate ///boat.plums.modes
Cafes/pubs Pub at the start
Transport Limited bus service between Tavistock and Newton Abbot stops at Warren House Inn
Parking Two small parking areas near Warren House Inn on B3212 (PL20 6TA)
Toilets No public toilets on route

Time 2hr
Distance 6.5km (4 miles)
Climb 210m

An interesting walk with old mine workings, an ancient site and a medieval wayside cross

From the Warren House Inn follow a bridleway down to a stream before heading up past the ruins of the Birch Tor and Vitifer Mine. After passing Headland Warren Farm the route continues over open moor to Grimspound. A short steep ascent brings you to Hookney Tor. After admiring the view, continue along the Two Moors Way over open moor to Bennett's Cross. From here it's an easy walk back to the Warren House Inn.

The Warren House Inn

SHORT WALKS DARTMOOR NORTH

1 The 19th-century Warren House Inn is the highest pub in southern England at 434m above sea level. Facing the **Warren House Inn**, turn right alongside the road (B3212) for 200m to a small parking area on the right. Turn half-right through the **car park** and follow the track (bridleway) heading away from the road. As the track curves left, fork right (straight on) down the narrow bridleway passing some ruins of the former **Vitifer Mine**.

> The once expansive Birch Tor and Vitifer Mine complex, which closed in the early 20th century, was said to have been one of the most profitable tin mines on Dartmoor.

2 Cross the clapper bridge over the stream, turn right for a few paces to a Y-junction and fork left. Follow the bridleway uphill, with a stone wall on the right for a time, and pass more old mine workings. After crossing the saddle continue downhill for 400m, passing just left of a stone wall to a junction near **Headland Warren Farm**. Turn left and immediately fork right at the Y-junction, heading up a narrow path to a **minor road**.

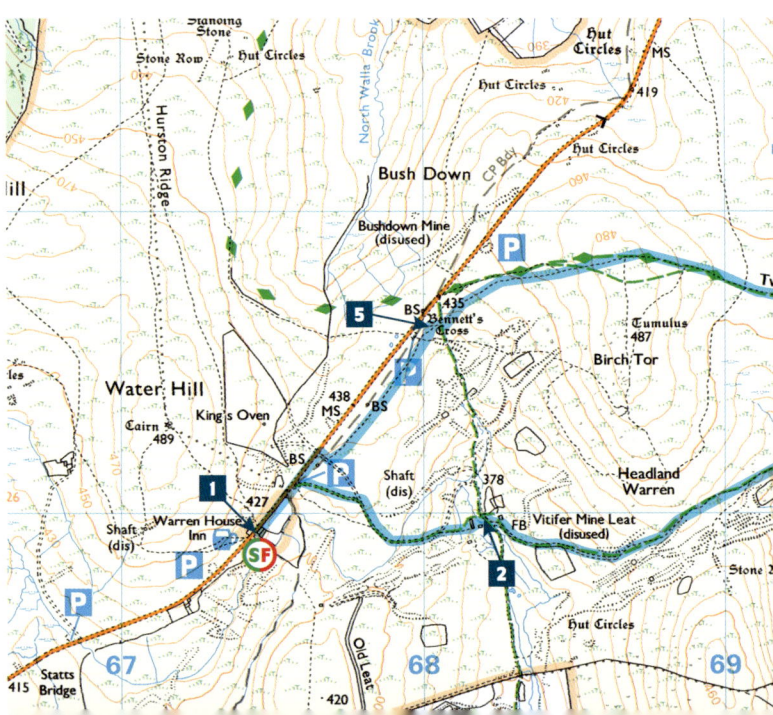

Hut circle at Grimspound looking towards Hookney Tor

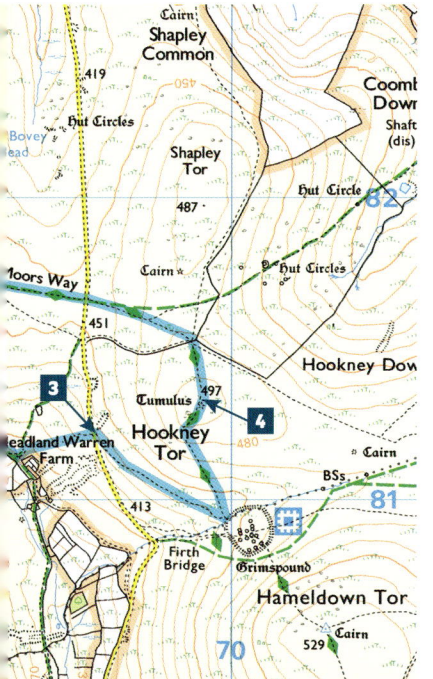

3 Cross over and bear right on a narrow path contouring round the hill to a stream. Just across the stream is **Grimspound**.

This impressive Bronze Age settlement, built around 3500–3000 years ago, is one of Dartmoor's best-known prehistoric sites. Contained within the large 150m diameter boundary wall, which has a paved and stone-faced entrance on the southern side, are the remains of 24 stone roundhouses.

The onward route turns left following the **Two Moors Way** all the way to Bennett's Cross. Continue up the path to the outcrops of **Hookney Tor**

The route passes old gateposts shortly after leaving Hookney Tor

(497m). Views include Hameldown Tor and Grimspound behind you; to the left is Challacombe Down and Birch Tor, with the Warren House Inn visible between them.

4 Head to the highest outcrop and continue along the wide path (Two Moors Way) heading towards a stone wall and go between the two old gateposts. Here the route splits three-ways, bear half-left following the middle route (Two Moors Way) downhill. Cross the minor road and continue in the same direction up to the brow of the hill. A path to the left leads to Birch Tor (487m) – another good viewpoint (350m each way). Keep ahead down to **Bennett's Cross**, which stands near a small car park; the walk leaves the Two Moors Way here.

> Bennett's Cross is a rather mishappen medieval wayside cross. It may be a Christianised prehistoric standing stone. It was later used as a boundary stone between the parishes of Chagford and North Bovey and as a boundary marker for Headland Warren.

Bennett's Cross

5 At the cross turn left, pass some 15m to the left of the **car park** and continue along a path parallel with the road. On reaching a track, turn right to the road and then turn left along the verge back to the **Warren House Inn**.

WALK 13
Bellever Tor

Start/finish	*Postbridge National Park Visitor Centre*
Locate	*///blubber.tiredness.gratitude*
Cafes/pubs	*Pub and shop/tea room at Postbridge*
Transport	*Buses from Yelverton, Tavistock and Newton Abbott stop at Postbridge*
Parking	*Pay-and-display car park beside visitor centre or Bellever Forest car park (both PL20 6TH)*
Toilets	*At visitor centre*

Time 2¼hr
Distance 7km (4¼ miles)
Climb 200m

Take a walk along forestry tracks, visit some ancient sites and climb up a tor for a view

From Postbridge you follow tracks up through Bellever Forest, making a brief detour to visit an ancient stone row and cist. The walking soon gets a bit more interesting as you head up a stony path to Bellever Tor. After admiring the view it's off downhill before following the Lych Way for a while. The final leg takes you along forestry tracks back towards the visitor centre. Make time to visit the medieval clapper bridge at Postbridge at the end of the walk.

The stony path leading up towards Bellever Tor

SHORT WALKS DARTMOOR NORTH

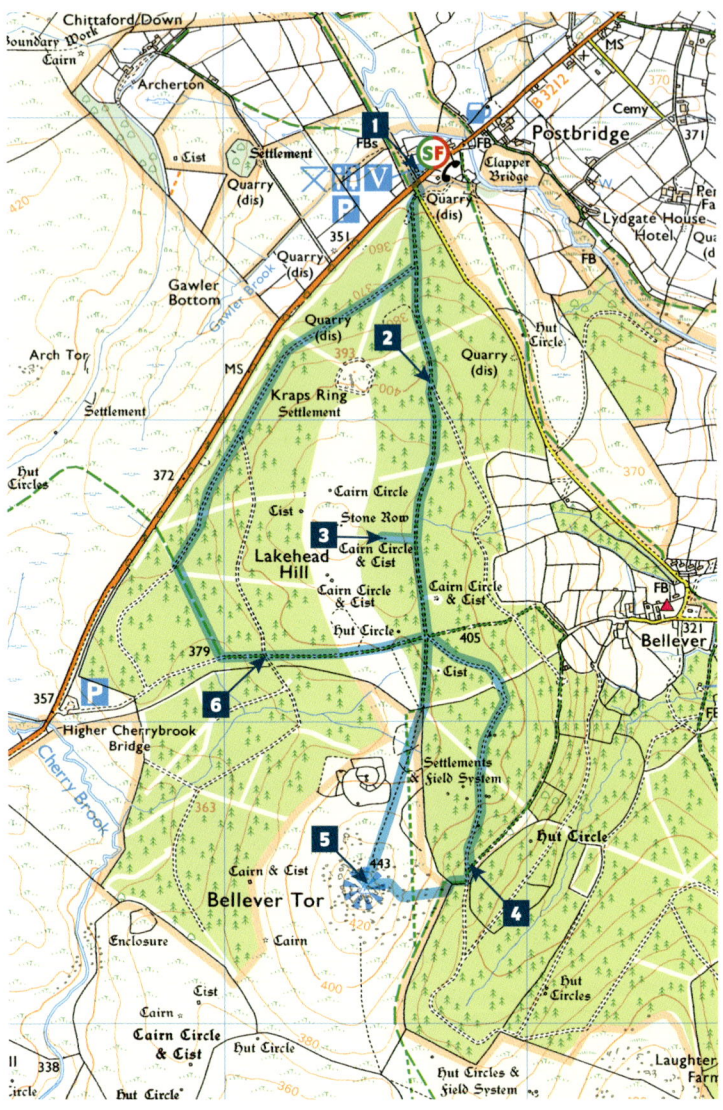

The stone row and cist on Lakehead Hill

1 Take the path at the top of the car park just to the left of the visitor centre at **Postbridge**. Turn left, cross the **B3212** and take the lane opposite towards Bellever. After passing the cattle grid, fork right on a track and then keep left of the Bellever Forest car park (alternative start point). Go through the gate and follow the track up to a Y-junction. Fork left and follow the track up to another Y-junction.

2 Fork right along the fairly level track for 500m to a path on the right. Turn right along this towards the summit of Lakehead Hill to visit a **stone row and cist**. The Bronze Age cist and stone row is one of a number of ancient sites that can be found on Lakehead Hill.

3 Return to the track and turn right to a five-way junction, then take the second turn on the left. For a shorter walk turn right along the bridleway. Follow the track through an open area. As the track starts to descend there is a Bronze Age hut circle a few paces left of the track. Continue down to a track junction.

4 Keep ahead for 15m and then turn right up a stony path beside an old wall. At the corner turn left for 20m and then turn right. Follow the path up to **Bellever Tor** (443m).

SHORT WALKS DARTMOOR NORTH

Summit of Bellever Tor

Bellever Tor has a great view: look to the large mast above Princetown and moving right (clockwise) there is Beardown Tors, Higher White Tor, Rough Tor and Cut Hill, then Sittaford Tor (north); continuing round is the broad outline of Hamel Down, then Haytor Rocks, Rippon Tor and Ryder's Hill (south).

5 On reaching the tor turn right and follow a wide path downhill to an old wall. Keep ahead along the track to the five-way junction visited earlier and turn left. This is the Lych Way used by residents of the small farmsteads in the surrounding area so that they could bury their dead at Lydford parish church. Follow the bridleway to a crossing track.

6 Cross straight over and continue down the bridleway to a junction. Turn right between earth banks to a crossing track. Turn right along the track for slightly under 1.5km, ignoring a side track on the right, to reach a track junction. Turn left downhill, retracing your steps past the car park (left) to the lane. Turn left and cross the **B3212** back to the visitor centre.

To visit the picturesque medieval clapper bridge turn right along the pavement (B3212) down past the bus stop and village shop/tea room, then cross over the road and follow the path to the East Dart River and the clapper bridge.

The medieval clapper bridge and road bridge at Postbridge

– To shorten

To miss out the climb up Bellever Tor, at the five-way junction turn right and follow the bridleway (Lych Way) to a track junction, then continue from Waypoint 6. This reduces the walk by 2km (45min) and saves 80m climbing.

Hameldown Beacon and boundary stone

WALK 14
Widecombe in the Moor

Start/finish	*Widecombe in the Moor village green*
Locate	*///burn.colder.trifling*
Cafes/pubs	*Pubs and tea room at Widecombe in the Moor*
Transport	*Limited Saturday bus service from Newton Abbot*
Parking	*Pay-and-display parking near village green in Widecombe in the Moor (TQ13 7TA)*
Toilets	*At car park*

Time 2¼hr
Distance 6.5km (4 miles)
Climb 275m

Explore a picturesque village and then make a fairly lengthy climb up to Hameldown Beacon for the views

From Widecombe in the Moor – which is well worth exploring at the beginning of your walk – it's a steady and at times steep climb onto the open moor of Hamel Down. Then it's off along the Two Moors Way up to the lofty heights of Hameldown Beacon. After admiring the views you retrace your steps for a while before heading downhill – steeply at times – back to the village green.

The Church House with loggia and the church tower at Widecombe in the Moor

85

SHORT WALKS DARTMOOR NORTH

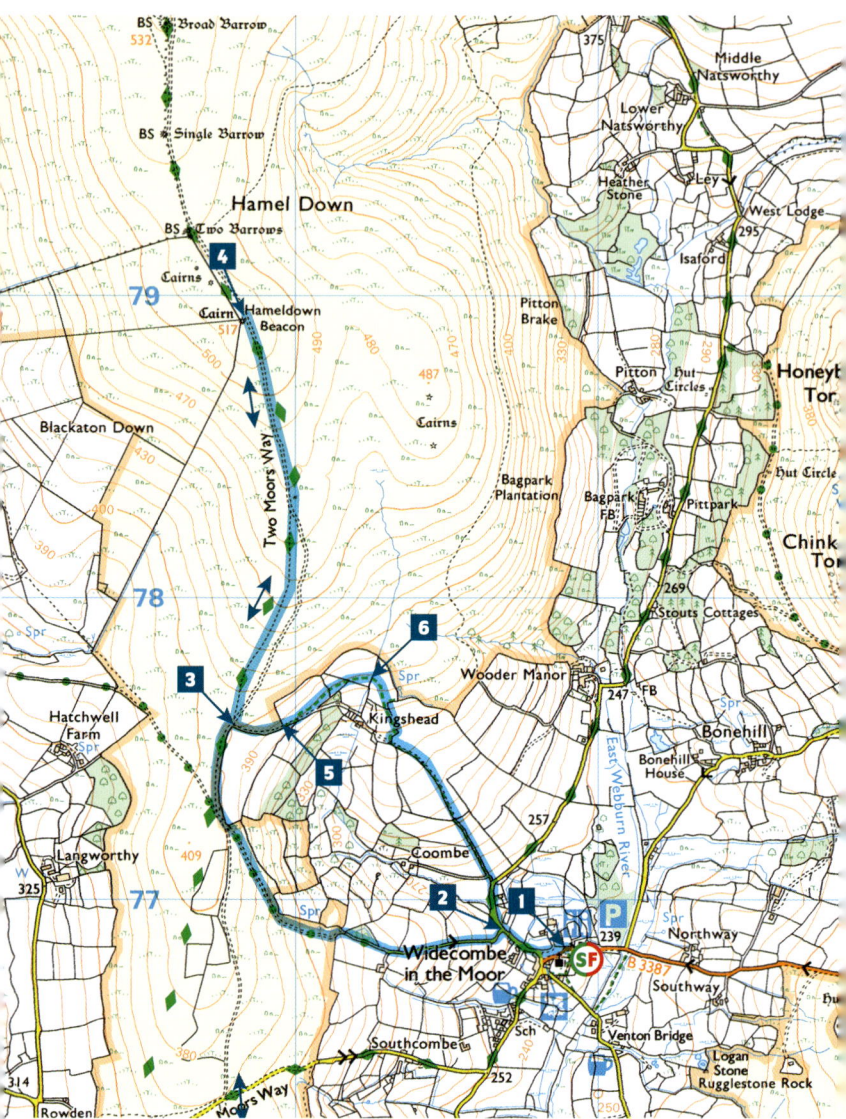

WALK 14 – WIDECOMBE IN THE MOOR

Cafe on the Green at Widecombe in the Moor

1 At the village green in **Widecombe in the Moor**, face the church with the tea room behind you and turn right following the path alongside the village green, which is on your left, to a road.

The onward route bears right but to explore the village first, turn left to a junction, keep right for a few paces with the Old Inn on your right, and turn left alongside the Church House. Through the lych gate is St Pancras' Church, and 350m along the lane is the Rugglestone Inn.

Turn right in the direction of Natsworthy. Follow the lane for 150m and turn left along a tarmac track signed 'Footpath for Grimspound via Hameldown'.

2 Follow the tarmac track steeply uphill and on nearing some buildings (left), bear right along the enclosed track. Go through a gate onto the open moor and follow the track uphill as it swings left and right to a junction. Keep right, following the **Two Moors Way** with a wall on your right to a wall corner. For the shorter route turn right here.

3 Keep ahead, following the Two Moors Way uphill for 1.5km to **Hameldown Beacon**, beside a wall on your left. For a longer walk keep ahead.

> ⓘ *The Two Moors Way, a 188km long-distance coast-to-coast route from Lynmouth to Wembury (in South Devon), meanders through Dartmoor.*

87

Along Hamel Down are several Bronze Age cairns, or burial mounds, topped with boundary stones marking the Duke of Somerset's land, carved with 'DS 1854'. The view from Hameldown Beacon includes Haytor Rocks, and on a clear day you can see the Isle of Portland 100km away.

4 Now turn around and retrace your steps back down to the corner of the wall (Waypoint 3) and take the second path on the left alongside the wall on your right to a gate.

5 Go through the gate leaving the open moor and head down the track. Bear left through a gate into the field and follow the right-hand boundary. Cross a stile and continue through the next field to another stile. Continue through a third field and cross a footbridge and ladder stile to the left of the field corner.

6 Continue down the wide path, keeping ahead at a junction, and go through a gate. Turn left down the steep track. At the bottom go through a gate and turn right along the lane back to the village green in **Widecombe in the Moor**.

> *Explore 5000 years of life on Dartmoor from the Bronze Age through to the mid-20th century at the Museum of Dartmoor Life in Okehampton (www.dartmoorlife.org.uk).*

Heading along the track towards the open moor

Following the Two Moors Way up Hamel Down

Widecombe in the Moor

Picturesque Widecombe in the Moor is home to a fair on the second Tuesday of September, immortalised in the folk song 'Widecombe Fair' along with 'Old Uncle Tom Cobley and All'. The 14th-century Perpendicular-style Church of St Pancras is known locally as the 'Cathedral of the Moor'. Its lofty tower was added in the 16th century. The Church House, with its loggia, dates from the 16th century.

▬ To shorten

At Waypoint 3 turn right alongside the wall to a gate and continue from Waypoint 5. This reduces the walk by 3km (60min) and saves 110m climbing.

✚ To lengthen

From Hameldown Beacon continue along the broad ridge, passing Two Barrows and Single Barrow to arrive at Broad Barrow. Then turn around and retrace your steps. This adds 2km (45min).

Haytor Quarry

WALK 15
Haytor Rocks

Start/finish	*Haytor National Park Visitor Centre*
Locate	*///offers.dignitary.bounded*
Cafes/pubs	*Pub at Haytor Vale (400m off route)*
Transport	*Limited bus service between Bovey Tracey and Newton Abbot, also Haytor Hoppa bus (summer Saturdays only)*
Parking	*Pay-and-display car park at Haytor Visitor Centre on B3387 (TQ13 9XT)*
Toilets	*At visitor centre*

Time 1¾hr
Distance 5km (3 miles)
Climb 150m

A popular tor, lots of views, old quarries and a fascinating granite tramway

This varied walk takes you up to Haytor Quarries before continuing up to Haytor Rocks – one of Dartmoor's best-known and most-visited tors. Then it's off down to Holwell Tor for a great view before heading downhill to join the old granite tramway. You then follow the tramway – part of the Templer Way – back towards Haytor Vale and the visitor centre.

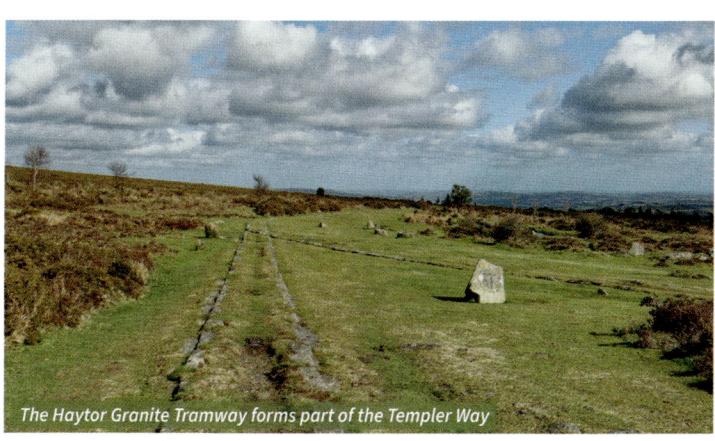

The Haytor Granite Tramway forms part of the Templer Way

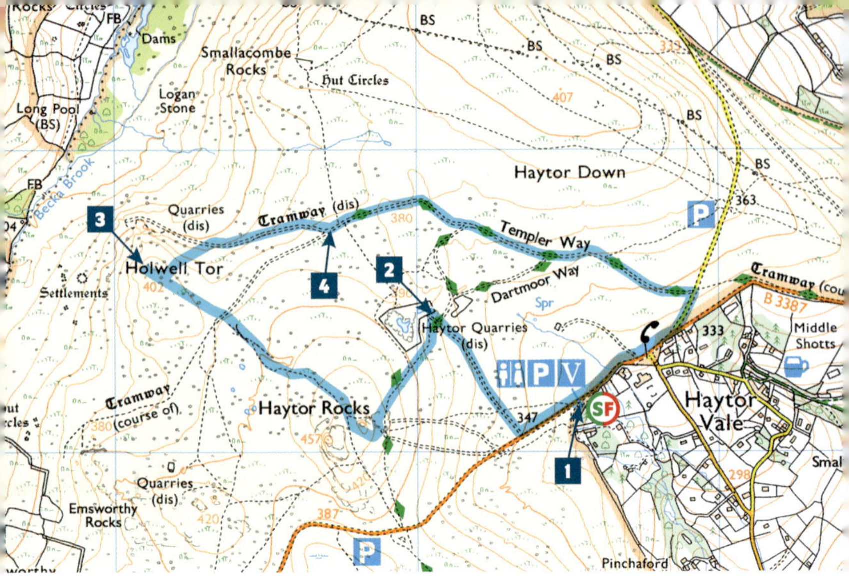

1 From the visitor centre at **Haytor** head over to the car park entrance/exit and cross over the B3387. Turn left alongside the road for 200m and then turn right along a track (the prominent Haytor Rocks are up diagonally left). Continue up the track to a gate that gives access to **Haytor Quarries**. The onward route turns left; however, before that go through the gate and follow the path to the left to explore the old quarry.

> The largest of the five quarries in the area, Haytor Quarry was worked from the late 18th century until the 1860s. Take care, the flooded quarry is unfenced.

The impressive rock stack of Haytor Rocks

Looking along the grassy path that leads from Haytor Rocks down to Holwell Tor

> ⓘ **The world-famous author Agatha Christie, dubbed the 'Queen of crime', stayed at the Moorland Hotel at Haytor whilst writing her first novel** A Mysterious Affair at Styles.

2 Return through the gate and turn right. Follow the path up towards **Haytor Rocks**. Pass clockwise (left) round the dome-shaped outcrop and keep right to a grassy area between the two large outcrops that make up Haytor Rocks. Views include southwards over the South Hams, the Teign Valley and the coast, and northwards to Hound Tor. Keep ahead (heading away from the road) and follow a path downhill, later passing to the left of a quarry to a path junction. Keep ahead, passing just left of the quarry spoil heaps, and continue over fairly flat ground to **Holwell Tor** (402m).

The tor makes a good picnic spot and has some nice views, including north over the Becka Brook valley to the jagged outcrops of Hound Tor and Greater Rocks, whilst behind you is Haytor Rocks.

3 From the main summit turn around and retrace your steps for 20m to a path junction, then turn left down a wide grassy path to a track and the granite **tramway**. Turn right up this (left leads to Holwell Quarry) to a tramway junction and keep left. For a longer walk turn left at this junction.

Templer Way marker stone

4 Continue following the tramway. Later another tramway joins from the right beside a marker stone for the **Templer Way**. Keep ahead to reach a minor road. Turn right down the road to a junction with the **B3387**. Turn right alongside the road back to the visitor centre, which is on the left, across the road.

For a pub visit, once level with the road junction on the left, turn left across the road. Follow the lane to a junction – the Moorland Hotel is on the right – and turn left in the direction of Haytor Vale down to the Rock Inn, then retrace your steps. This adds 800m (20min).

+ To lengthen

At Waypoint 4 turn left and follow a path out to Smallacombe Rocks (another nice viewpoint). Turn around, retrace your route back to the tramway and turn left to continue the walk. This adds 1km (25min).

Haytor Granite Tramway

The unique granite tramway was built by George Templer using granite rails (rather than iron rails) to guide the wheels of horse-drawn wagons. The tramway, which opened in 1820, was used to transport granite from the quarries at Haytor down to Ventiford Quay on the Stover Canal, southeast of Bovey Tracey, before being transported by barge to Newton Abbot and then on to Teignmouth. The 27km long Templer Way, named after the Templer family who also built the 18th-century Stover Canal, follows the tramway, canal and River Teign from Haytor down to Teignmouth.

USEFUL INFORMATION

Tourism bodies

Dartmoor National Park
www.dartmoor.gov.uk
Visit Dartmoor
www.visitdartmoor.co.uk

Tourist information centres

National Park visitor centres
Princetown, tel 01822 890414
Haytor, tel 0364 661520
Postbridge, tel 01822 880272

Local information centres
Ashburton, tel 01364 653426
Bovey Tracey, tel 01626 832047
Ivybridge, tel 01752 897035
Moretonhampstead, tel 01647 440043
Okehampton, tel 01837 52295
Tavistock, tel 01822 813946

Travel

Train enquiries
National Rail
www.nationalrail.co.uk

Bus timetables
Traveline
www.traveline.info

Other contacts

Livestock incidents
All livestock, including ponies, are owned by local farmers and commoners. If you come across injured livestock please phone the Livestock Protection Officer, tel 07873 587561.

Databases on Dartmoor tors and sites
The Tors of Dartmoor
www.torsofdartmoor.co.uk
Dartefacts
www.dartefacts.co.uk

© Steve Davison 2025
First edition 2025
ISBN: 978 1 78631 191 7
eISBN: 978 1 78765 174 6

Printed in Singapore by KHL Printing on responsibly sourced paper.
A catalogue record for this book is available from the British Library.
All photographs are by the author unless otherwise stated.
Cover illustration of Scorhill Circle by Avery Mitchell.

© Crown copyright and database rights 2025 OS AC0000810376

CICERONE

Cicerone Press, Juniper House, Murley Moss, Oxenholme Road, Kendal, Cumbria, LA9 7RL

www.cicerone.co.uk

Updates to this Guide

While every effort is made to ensure the accuracy of guidebooks as they go to print, changes can occur during the lifetime of an edition. Any updates that we know of for this guide will be on the Cicerone website (www.cicerone.co.uk/1191/updates), so please check before planning your trip. We also advise that you check information about transport, accommodation and shops locally. Even rights of way can be altered over time. We are always grateful for information about any discrepancies between a guidebook and the facts on the ground, sent by email to updates@cicerone.co.uk.

Register your book: To sign up to receive free updates, special offers and GPX files where available, create a Cicerone account and register your purchase via the 'My Account' tab at www.cicerone.co.uk.